To my wife Lori for making
my life exponentially better.
To Bryn, Noah, and Lila
for filling my heart with joy.

ISBN 9780578699127

eISBN 9780578707266

EVERYTHING IS BETTER THAN YOU THINK

HOW GRATITUDE CAN TRANSFORM YOUR LIFE

WILL JOHNS

CONTENTS

PREFACE

In the summer of 2012, one Sunday morning, I drove the 1½ hour drive from my home to Portland, Oregon, for the sole purpose of seeing my nephew, Will. Living on opposite sides of the country made it more difficult to keep in touch and since he was attending a meeting in Portland, what better opportunity to catch up! I'm glad I did. It was a life-changing get-together. Indeed, it was more than just catching up. It led to moving forward with a whole new perspective on life.

During the course of our lunch together at the Old Spaghetti Factory, I found out he was pursuing a doctoral degree with a focus on the subject of gratitude. His enthusiasm for the topic was infectious and the more he explained to me what tremendous impact gratitude (or the lack thereof) has on the quality of our lives, the more I knew I needed to incorporate it into my own life. While we only had time to scratch the surface, that spark ignited a fire that has made all the difference in the world to me.

I took the few tidbits he shared with me. I accessed some of the resources he pointed out to me. And I applied the principles I was learning to my own experiences. I began looking at virtually everything through a new lens (an appropriate metaphor for an ophthalmologist), the lens of being grateful, and I began seeing things in a new and different light. And it was a much brighter light.

I discovered that indeed, Everything is Better Than You Think. I discovered how there are far more good things to focus on in my life than bad things. But above all, I discovered the happiness of gratitude. There is a new joy. There is so much more to appreciate and revel in. The colors are brighter. The smiles are bigger and the laughs more frequent.

Gratitude has changed my life in a miraculous way. I was fortunate to first and foremost recognize my need for a change, and then to find the keys to that change. Indeed, I am now tremendously grateful for gratitude. It not only can, but it will change your life too, if only you allow it. I'm living proof that it works. Wherever you are in your life journey, gratitude can make a difference for you. I hope that you too will find this same happiness and joy that a life of gratitude brings.

—Gordon Johns, MD, Ophthalmologist, Chehalis WA

INTRODUCTION

What if I could give you a pair of magical glasses that changed the way you saw the world? What if whenever you wore these glasses you felt much better? In fact, let's say the glasses are powerful enough to turn a bad day into a good day. In fact, they are powerful enough to change despair into hope. And these glasses only cost a few dollars. Interested? Most people would probably want to buy these glasses. The good news for you is that you already have! This book can have the same effect as magical glasses, except that it doesn't work through magic. You will be taught how to be intentional about what you focus on and it will transform the way you feel. The world outside will remain as it is. But what you see there, will be radically different.

Your life is actually much better than you think it is. How could I possibly know that about you? This assertion is based on solid research showing that the human mind naturally focuses on negative things. When you focus on the negative things in your life, you are going to feel bad and believe your life is bad. But in reality, there are many good things happening in your life that you just can't see yet because your attention is directed towards the bad stuff. This is where my magical glasses come in. I'm going to teach you in the following pages how you can start to see the good that is already in your life. This will cause you to feel much better. In addition, it will give you a more accurate view of reality.

This book was born of my own journey. It began as an academic pursuit. For three years, I've immersed myself in the study of the subject of gratitude, working toward my Doctoral Degree. What I discovered absolutely amazed me. Research shows we can be significantly happier without anything external changing in our lives. And the more positive we feel after practicing gratitude, the more likely we are to make better decisions. Thus, gratitude does not only make us happier in the present, it also has real, practical power to help us choose a better future as well.

Sound too good to be true? Too easy? I can offer some reassurance here—gratitude is not an easy practice. But the concept is extremely simple and can be practiced by anyone. You don't need a doctoral degree or three years of study to benefit from what I am about to share with you. Just an openness to learn something new and a willingness to try applying it to your life. If you do, I am confident you will see amazing results. This book has the power to transform your life if you are willing to put it into prac-

tice. Pretty soon, you will be wearing these magical glasses all the

time!

CHAPTER ONE
CHANGING THE LENS

"Gratitude is not only the greatest,
but the parent of all the other virtues."

M. T. Cicero,

The Orations of Marcus Tullius Cicero

One day in eighth grade, I woke up and realized that my world looked like a Monet painting. Everything far away was blurry. The change had happened so slowly it took me a while to notice I couldn't read the blackboard in my classroom at school. So, my parents took me to the eye doctor, and he prescribed glasses for me. I still remember how awestruck I was when I put them on. Suddenly, everything was clear once again. The problem was I thought the glasses were ugly and embarrassing to wear. Fortunately, my parents soon agreed to let me get contact lenses. When I finally overcame my fear of putting something into my eyes and got the contacts in after a frustrating hour of trial and error,

I was completely overwhelmed. Not only was everything clear, but I didn't even see the edges of lenses in my peripheral vision. Those tiny little lenses I placed on my eyes every morning changed everything for me. The world looked completely different.

That's exactly what gratitude can do in your life. Gratitude is a lens that changes the perception of everything in your life. Your world will be transformed. You will begin to see good things you've never noticed before. You will begin to feel joy for things in your life you knew were good but never fully appreciated. You will be able to count your blessings even during difficult circumstances. Gratitude will affect your essential perspective of and attitude toward life. And it will bring you the happiness you have been seeking your entire life.

However, it doesn't happen naturally. This is a skill you will have to work towards. The good news is this: It is much easier to learn how to practice gratitude than it is to put contacts in your eyes. Although, if I could figure out how to manufacture gratitude contact lenses, I would probably become a rich man! In my research, I discovered there are some very simple habits that, once formed, reoriented me toward thankfulness. These habits are easily taught and can be implemented right away. We will look at how to develop good gratitude habits in chapter 8.

The reason gratitude can be so difficult is explained by neuroscience research, showing the brain—when it's not actively engaged in the present moment—defaults to finding fault with oneself, others, or one's situation. This helps to explain why individuals tend to focus on the negative in their lives more than on their blessings—since the brain naturally wanders from the present moment 46 percent of the time. You have probably had this experience yourself. You are driving down the road, and all of a sudden you realize you feel terrible. What is going on? You trace your thoughts back and discover in your mental wanderings you subconsciously decided to settle on something painful to think about.

Now before we get too upset at our minds for doing this to us, we need to realize that our minds have a reason for looking for the negative. They are trying to protect us from danger. So, we do well by being alert, say, to potential hazards on the road around us or the health and safety of our families. However, this pattern becomes unhelpful when we are in safe situations and yet feeling bad, because our minds are focused on the negative things in our lives.

Complicating the matter further, neuroscientists have now discovered that negative experiences are like Velcro—they stick in our minds instantly. But positive experiences are like Teflon, and they only stick if we savor the experience for at least 15 seconds. (This is another vital reason to develop gratitude habits, but we'll talk more about that in Chapter 8). And if we aren't proactive, we will steadily become more negative as we get older.

This is what I've discovered when I delved deep into the research:

"In the absence of conscious efforts to engage, build, and sustain positive perceptions and emotions, we all too automatically fall prey to feelings such as irritation, anxiety, worry, frustration, judgmentalness, self-doubt, and blame. As negative feelings are repeatedly rehashed, these patterns reinforce their familiarity in the neural architecture, thus becoming stereotyped and increasingly automatic and mechanical. Many people do not realize the extent to which these habitual response patterns dominate their internal landscape, diluting and limiting positive emotional experience and eventually becoming so familiar that they become engrained in one's sense of self-identity."

The real danger of not recognizing our minds' tendency to grow negative is that we can ultimately end up with a negative sense of identity. We may begin to feel like "a born loser" or "a failure" or worse.

As a pastor, I have had the opportunity to get to know a large number of people in their 80s and 90s. I am fascinated by this age group, because they show us so clearly the final fruition of the habits we form when we are young. In my limited observation, I have noticed two types of people in these age categories. The first type is bitter and full of resentment. Nothing is ever good enough for them. When I listen to their stories, I am told about count-less heartaches and strained relationships with their spouses and children. I am told how they had been mistreated by others and that nothing ever seemed to go their way. They are angry about their health struggles. In short, they are miserable people. And, if I am honest, I want to get away from them as quickly as possible. I feel myself being sucked into the black hole of their negativity. Ingratitude is contagious, by the way, and we do need to monitor and limit our exposure to it.

I'm glad to tell you I have also met many examples of a sec-ond type of person advanced in years. These people radiate joy and peace. I go to visit them because of health problems they face, and they are always the ones to cheer me up. They ask me about my life, how I am doing. They laugh and tell stories about how blessed they are. They have great relationships with others. They are at peace with themselves, with God and with life in gener-al. They've developed a life-long habit of looking for the good in their lives and appreciating it and being thankful for it. As a re-sult, over time, they've become more and more grateful.

I'd like you to imagine for a moment, two parallel lines mov-ing away from you like railroad tracks. Except that they are one degree wider than parallel. At first, they won't seem to be much different. But the further those tracks go, the wider apart they be-come. The set of lines on the left illustrates what the tracks would look like at the beginning. The lines on the right show how much further apart they would get further down the track. This explains the major difference I've observed in the older people I've met. The longer we practice a habit, the more it affects who we are.

Whatever we focus on, we will get more of. When we focus on what we don't like, we will get more of what we don't like. When we focus on what we are grateful for, we will end up with more to be grateful for. Over time, we will begin to tell ourselves a story about ourselves. It is of utmost importance to be intentional about this process. If we tell ourselves a negative story, such as, "I'm cursed" or, "Nothing ever goes my way," then we will begin to look for all of the things in life that confirm this story. This is called confirmation bias in the research. The negative story creates a negative focus, which results in negative feelings. Those negative feelings reinforce the negative story and so the bitter cycle continues.

This negative cycle is reversible, however. You don't have to be stuck in it for life. If we intentionally tell ourselves a good story about ourselves, like "I am fortunate," or, "I've been given so many good things in life," then our minds will naturally begin to look for evidence to confirm this point of view. We will start noticing more and more of the good things in our lives, and the blessed story will be reinforced in a wonderful cycle of gratitude. When I met some of the grateful saints, I was convinced I needed to learn their secret. And now I am even more convinced that I need to put the power of gratitude to work in my life. But what does that look like?

When I was 21, I had the great privilege of traveling to Brazil as part of a short-term mission group. We took a boat 24 hours into the Amazon jungle in order to do medical work, build a church, and conduct activities for the children in the village. This was an amazing adventure where we saw crocodiles, piranhas, monkeys, and sloths. But what impressed me most was meeting a boy who was probably seven years old. He lived in a primitive hut. His entire wardrobe was a pair of well-worn shorts. He owned just one toy. It was a primitive-looking top—a piece of wood carved into a rough cone shape with a piece of string. He would wrap the string around the top and throw it on the ground, hanging onto the string at the other end. As he watched the top spinning, the look on his face was one of pure joy. I have rarely witnessed this rapture among children in the United States. And yet, most of the children I have met in America have thousand times as much!

The point is this: what you see determines what you feel. If your mind is focused on what you don't have, you will experience emptiness, sorrow and longing. If your mind—like the boy in Brazil—is focused on what you do have, then joy is the automatic result.

Ultimately, gratitude is about focus. It is a choice to intentionally focus on what is good in my life. Even though it can be a struggle—since our minds tend to gravitate towards the negative—we are not doomed to become negative people. We still have the power of choice. I believe God has given us that power of choice, and no one can take it away. The good news is that it is never too late to start choosing gratitude. When we choose to be thankful, we are choosing to live a richer life, a more fulfilling life. And if you are a parent, you are choosing to transmit the power of gratitude to the next generation by modeling for your children the behavior you want to see displayed in their lives.

Are you ready to get really motivated? Let's look at the many benefits you receive by forming a habit of gratitude.

CHAPTER 2
THE BENEFITS OF GRATITUDE

I recently came back from a business trip to Orlando, and I wanted to buy something for my son I thought he would like. When I tell you what I purchased for him, please don't judge me as a parent. I just knew my ten-year-old son would be excited to get this. What was it that I saw in the gift shop and purchased for Noah? Sour cream and onion crickets. The number one ingredient in this tasty snack? Crickets. That's right, the insect. Not some cricket-shaped crackers. Real dead, dried crickets. Pretty disgusting really. My wife was horrified when she found out what I had done. But Noah was so excited to show his friends. And of course, being ten-year-old boys, they all had to try one just to be able to comment on how gross they were!

Now I want you to imagine sitting down for a meal at your favorite restaurant. The waiter brings you two plates. One plate is your favorite dish at this restaurant. Go ahead. Imagine what this looks like, tastes like, smells like. Hungry? I bet you are! Now imagine receiving a second plate full of sour cream and onion crickets. Looks disgusting. Now here's the point I'm trying to make. You have a choice in this moment about what you are going to eat. Do you want to eat the crickets? Of course not! (Unless, like my son, you have a kind of morbid curiosity about what they might taste like.) But, for the sake of the illustration, let's say you go ahead and eat one of the crickets, and it really is as gross as it looked. Now, you have a choice again—keep eating the crickets or push the plate of crickets to one side and eat and savor your favorite dish. It is an easy choice in this context. Of course, you'll eat your favorite food.

But the reality is, we face this type of choice every day. Gratitude is the good meal, one to enjoy and savor. And yet, we are more likely to choose the crickets. Why is this? It is not because you are a bad person. It is because you are a person, a human being. And as we have looked at the last chapter, the human mind naturally focuses on the negative. However, with a little training, you can change those mental patterns so that you naturally choose gratitude (the good meal) instead of negative thoughts (the crickets). Once the habit of gratitude is firmly in place in your mind, the desire to indulge in negative thinking will lose its hold on you. We will look at why our minds gravitate towards the negative more indepth in the next chapter. For now, all you need to know is that you have a choice in this matter, and you can choose gratitude!

I hope to convince you that choosing gratitude is well worth it on many levels. In fact, I have come to believe that gratitude is a "hinge habit" in life. A hinge habit is a routine that allows the development of other good habits as a result. Exercise is a hinge habit for most people. You could view gratitude as a foundational habit upon which to build other positive practices. The point is this: lots of good things can come into your life through this one simple practice. Let's look at all of those benefits now.

First of all, gratitude leads to an overall sense of well-being. Listen to what the research shows: "A grateful response to life circumstances may be an adaptive psychological strategy and an important process by which people positively interpret everyday experiences. The ability to notice, appreciate, and savor the elements of one's life has been viewed as a crucial determinant of well-being." The importance of gratitude to well-being is almost self-evident. However, the human brain is so likely to focus on the negative, this obvious truth becomes obscured. If a person experiences something enjoyable in his or her life, the ability to savor that good experience is certainly an important skill to develop. This act of reflection is, in itself, a positive experience, which creates the sense that one's life is blessed. It also preserves the good memory for repeated enjoyment in the future.

Research has also shown that "participants in the gratitude condition reported getting more hours of sleep each night, spending less time awake before falling asleep and feeling more refreshed upon awakening." This further supports the evidence of gratitude promoting overall well-being.

The second major benefit of gratitude is that it increases our overall level of life satisfaction. The key element in this appears to be the focal point of the mind. The mind fixated on blessings is a satisfied mind, able to relax and sleep soundly at night. The individual waking up refreshed with good sleep is more likely to feel alive and revitalized. This prepares such an individual to have more to be grateful for in the future. And thus, a cycle of gratitude and well-being has begun. The research of Emmons and McCullough supports the concept of a positive gratitude cycle. "Gratitude not only makes people feel good in the present, but it also increases the likelihood that people will function optimally and feel good in the future."

Unlike some good habits, such as exercise, saving money or eating more healthfully, gratitude offers immediate and present impact while also serving as an investment in the future. Those future benefits received then give us more to be grateful for, and our minds are permeated with a sense of grace and well-being.

A friend of mine once spent some time working at a cancer treatment center. One thing she noticed as she spoke with patients is how happy and thankful they seemed during what, for many of them, was the worst time of their lives. They would talk more about the little joys of the day, or about friends and family who supported them or about how side effects were better than expected. They talked about how encountering this life-altering event had helped them discover how precious life was and choose to enjoy it. In doing so, they appreciated its value even more. Even, when in some cases, the patients had not been fully cured or the outcome was uncertain, my friend left these conversations feeling happy and inspired.

The front desk receptionist at the center, herself a survivor of stage-three breast cancer and undergoing regular treatment to keep the disease at bay, told her: "I don't let the little things bother me. I'm a more caring person. I don't worry about the future. I appreciate what I have right now." This is the power that gratitude has to change your perspective on any situation.

Additional research also backs up the assertion that gratitude creates a positive cycle of life satisfaction. Philip Watkins points out that, "self-report and non-self-report data converge to support the idea that grateful people tend to be happy people." The results of gratitude affect the whole person—both emotionally and physically. This leads to further feelings of subjective well-being. Watkins also discovered that "those in the grateful condition reported fewer health complaints and even said that they spent more time exercising than control participants did. Thus, a simple weekly intervention showed significant emotional and health benefits." All of these benefits promote health and a sound mind.

Consequently, it is not surprising to discover that gratitude also promotes mental health.

C.S. Lewis wrote that gratitude "seems to be inner health made audible." The literature clearly demonstrates a strong link between gratitude and mental health. However, we don't need research to convince us of this fact. We have all dealt with people who are so focused on the negative aspects of their lives that they cannot view the world around them clearly. This leads them to hold onto unbalanced and often self-destructive beliefs.

For example, my youngest daughter who was 7 years old at the time of this writing can really get herself into a negative state of self-pity at times. One of the rules in our household is that her room must be cleaned before she can watch TV. Not long ago, I asked her to clean her room. She said she didn't want to. I told her that was fine, but she would not be allowed to watch TV until her room was clean. Then she began to descend into the black hole of negativity. Through loud cries, she wailed, "It's not fair! I can't do it. I don't want to clean my room!" Pretty soon, she had worked herself up to, "Nobody loves me! I hate everybody!" Eventually, she calmed down, cleaned her room in 10 minutes and all was fine with her.

The child's dramatic outbursts actually give us an insight into our own more subtle "adult" ways of doing the same thing. I am given an assignment at work I don't feel like doing, and, by focusing on the negative, I get myself worked up to the point that I'm ready to quit my job and look for another one. Since a part of me knows how crazy this sounds, I generally am not quick to share my feelings with others in order to preserve my image as a mature adult. But the inner child still tries to throw his fits. How much better will it be if I make the conscious decision to look at the difficult task ahead of me as an exciting new challenge? When I focus on the good of the situation, my mental state immediately improves.

The ability to see reality and respond to it appropriately is one of the hallmarks of mental health. But when my mind is fixated only on the negative, reality is distorted since all the good in my life is being overlooked. As a result—like my daughter who despairs because of 10 minutes of work to clean her room—I may begin to see only problems with no solutions. Then life begins to feel "unfair" and before I know it, I may be convinced that "nobody loves me." These negative feelings must be faced for what they are. Gratitude does not create a shortcut by which we never feel something painful. But gratitude allows us to question the thoughts that accompany negative feelings, so they don't take over our way of thinking. (We'll look at this more in-depth in Chapter 5). So even if I have concluded that I need to quit my job—because I started down the black hole of negative thinking—gratitude helps steer me back to reality. I can say to myself, "I'm really feeling overwhelmed at work right now, but I'm thankful for a job that challenges me to push myself and achieve things that I didn't know I could do." Now I'm beginning to see the situation from a positive point of view, and I'm definitely much closer to seeing and dealing with reality in an effective way.

I cannot emphasize too strongly how much this aspect of gratitude can change your life. So much of our suffering is created in our minds (not all) and could be relieved by having a more realistic point of view that includes the positive elements of each situation we face. Over time, this creates a positive cycle of good decisions that produce good results that continually create more reasons to be grateful for what is happening in our lives.

The benefits of gratitude are clearly a prize worth pursuing; however, they do not come easily. I think we would all be incredibly grateful people if giving thanks came naturally to us. But we must face some very real obstacles to practicing gratitude. It is important to know what we are up against if we are going to overcome these barriers for us to realize the great benefits gratitude promises to bring into our lives. So now, let's look at what gets in the way of gratitude.

CHAPTER 3
WHAT GETS IN THE WAY?

A couple of years ago, with fear and trembling, I entered my first Spartan obstacle race. My brother had gotten himself into amazing shape, and he talked me into attempting one of these races. Our schedules did not allow for us to run together, so he completed the race before I began. When he called me, he warned me that the course was very difficult—4.5 miles long with 18 brutal obstacles. I began to question why I had foolishly signed up and paid money to torture myself. But my greatest fear was that I might not be able to finish. I had done a little running in preparation, but nothing more, so my fears were grounded in reality. About a mile into the race, they sent us crawling under barbed wire through mud almost 2 feet deep. It was pretty gross, but I made it. Around the halfway point, I was handed a 40-pound sandbag to shoulder for a quarter mile. I carried it downhill, into a creek bed, then began to start up the hill on the other side. I put the sandbag down to rest and was alarmed to discover that my heart rate wasn't coming back down. As I tried to catch my breath, I began to panic. I imagined taking the walk of shame back to the starting line and admitting defeat. The obstacles had beaten me! But after what felt like forever (probably only 5 minutes or so), I picked up the sandbag and finished the section. From that point on, I couldn't run without feeling short of breath, so I walked quickly instead. But I finished! And I have never felt so proud of myself for completing a race. I wore the medal they gave me at the end of the race like an Olympic gold. I wear the T-shirt that says "Finisher" with great pride to this day because I know what a great accomplishment that race was for me.

When it comes to gratitude, we are all going to face some daunting obstacles. But before we look at the major barriers to gratitude, I want to assure you that you can train yourself to overcome all of these obstacles. You may have your moments like I did in the Spartan race where you feel overwhelmed and are convinced you will not be able to get past this particular obstacle. Be gracious with yourself. Stop and reflect. Then just keep going. I promise you, gratitude is an even greater reward in itself than the Spartan medal I've received.

So, what are the obstacles to grateful living? There are three:

- The mind's tendency to default to negative thinking
- The vulnerability of joy
- A sense of entitlement

The Default to Negative Thinking

As we've already examined, our minds are not naturally programmed to support a gratitude habit. Remember from the first chapter, neuroscience research shows that the brain—when it is not actively engaged in the present moment—defaults to finding fault with oneself, others, or one's situation. And we tend to live outside the present moment with more focus on negative thoughts much of the time. This tendency can severely limit our ability to experience gratitude and joy. That's because negative thought patterns reinforce themselves. In the words of gratitude researchers Rollin McCraty and Doc Childre:

"In the absence of conscious efforts to engage, build, and sustain positive perceptions and emotions, we all too automatically fall prey to feelings such as irritation, anxiety, worry, frustration, judgmentalness, self-doubt, and blame. As negative feelings are repeatedly rehashed, these patterns reinforce their familiarity in the neural architecture, thus becoming stereotyped and increasingly automatic and mechanical. Many people do not realize the extent to which these habitual response patterns dominate their internal landscape, diluting and limiting positive emotional experience and eventually becoming so familiar that they become engrained in one's sense of self-identity."

As a result, over time, we can develop a pattern of replaying events that we regret. The reliving of painful experiences can cause us to remain stuck in the negativity of our past. The mind engages in critical thinking with the intention to work out problems. However, the negative emotions that accompany this default state of the mind often lead to self-destructive behavior. Our minds are well-established in the groove of trying to solve unsolvable problems. This leads to frustration and a feeling of helplessness as we try to figure out how to change what we cannot change. It is easy for people to be consumed with worries about the future or regrets about the past.

In contrast, "a person with gratitude-readiness will tend to see what is good in situations and notice less what is bad. The kinds of unfortunate actions and events that make the constitutionally regretful person miserable may have occurred in the grateful person's life as well, but the grateful person can move on from them, because his or her mind is tuned to happier things."

One of the ways to overcome the automatic default to negative thinking is to intentionally focus the mind on the present moment or the good things of the past. We empower ourselves when we engage in what is happening right now and center our thoughts on what can be changed in this moment. This is the simplest way to overcome this obstacle. However, we need to start with enough self-awareness to detect these bad feelings early on.

Emotions are always connected to thoughts. So, if you are feeling bad, you can be sure you are thinking something negative. However, you don't need to instantly solve the problem you are thinking about to feel good again. You can decide when you will work on that issue, maybe make a note on your calendar that you will deal with the problem at, say, 11 a.m. on Thursday. Then come back to the present moment or focus your mind intentionally on gratitude. Our emotions can really help us here. It is hard to ignore the discomfort of negative emotions, so sensing them can serve as a cue to come back to the present moment. We should do this gently, without being hard on ourselves. Sometimes, I have found it helpful to say, "Oh, there I go again, focusing on the negative. That's ok. Now that I'm aware of it, I can let those thoughts go and return to the present moment."

Let me add a balancing perspective. Practicing gratitude does not mean that we will never feel bad. It is very important to feel all of our emotions. The point is not to get stuck in negativity—especially imagined negativity. Feeling sadness when you experience an important loss in your life is appropriate, healthy and much needed. Feeling fear in a dangerous situation can help you stay alert and make better decisions. Feeling anger when your boundaries are crossed can motivate you to enforce good boundaries with others. Feeling guilt when you know you have harmed another person can lead you to try to make things right with them.

All of these negative emotions can serve a healthy role in our lives—as long as we feel them and then let them go. But when our minds betray us and fixate on the pain of our past, we are in danger of living a life of bitterness and regret. We are in danger of creating a negative self-identity, associated with thoughts like, "I'm cursed," or, "I'm a loser." The practice of gratitude keeps us from going down into the dark abyss and helps us to craft a positive self-identity such as "I'm blessed."

Kayla faced this obstacle head-on during her 22nd birthday. She had planned to meet her friends at a Jazz Club on the Saturday night of her birthday. She was looking forward to this all day and was extremely excited. Then she got some bad news. The Jazz group that she was expecting to play at the club was not going to be there. It was a Blues group instead. Suddenly the negative thoughts began in Kayla's mind. The whole point of going to that Jazz club was to hear the Jazz group. But now they won't be there. So, maybe I should go somewhere else. Nothing else sounded good to her. Her mind continued piling on negative thoughts. She no longer even felt like going out. Since she couldn't think of any restaurant she wanted to go to, she decided to cancel the whole party. She told her friends. They were very disappointed. She felt even worse. Then her mind went even further down into the abyss. "No one wants to be with you on your birthday. You're all alone." She was feeling terrible by now. Can you see how her mind was plunging her into darkness? Then she had the thought that saved her. She had recently attended a class on gratitude that I had taught and so she decided to take a moment to be grateful and see what might happen. She started thinking about how grateful she was for the friends she had in her life. She immediately felt better. She realized that these friends really wanted to be with her on her birthday and she felt even better. Then it dawned on her that she could still have a fun evening with them if she kept her original plans and decided to give the Blues group a chance. She called up her friends and had an amazing time with them that evening celebrating her birthday. She barely noticed the music because she felt so loved by her friends.

We can learn from Kayla's experience that our minds sometimes get stuck on some minor thing that absorbs our attention. The more we dwell on wanting to change what we can't change (in this case the music group) the more our brain will plunge us down into negativity. And worse yet, we may act upon these dark thoughts and make choices that are harmful to ourselves and others (canceling the party). But the choice to focus on gratitude can save us from unnecessary suffering as it did for Kayla.

So, now we have some tools in the bag to overcome this first and possibly most difficult obstacle. By feeling painful emotions and letting them go, we free ourselves to stay in the present moment. We also free our minds to be aware when we are starting to focus on the negative, and that awareness gives us a choice. We can now choose to come back to the present moment or focus on gratitude. And if we choose to do that on a consistent basis, we will strengthen our gratitude muscles and overcome the mind's tendency to focus on the negative.

The Vulnerability of Joy

We're over the first obstacle! Now, onto the vulnerability of joy. This was probably the most unexpected stumbling block to gratitude I've discovered in my research. Negative thinking was pretty obvious, but how could joy be an obstacle to gratitude? That sounds crazy! But here's is what I have uncovered.

Brené Brown, one of the leading researchers on the subject of vulnerability discovered that joy itself is an uncomfortable emotion for most people. Although it is a positive emotion, joy also puts people in touch with their deep-seated vulnerability.

"Joy is as thorny and sharp as any of the dark emotions. To love someone fiercely, to believe in something with your whole heart, to celebrate a fleeting moment in time, to fully engage in a life that doesn't come with guarantees—these are risks that involve vulnerability and often pain. When we lose our tolerance for discomfort, we lose joy. In fact, addiction research shows us that an intensely positive experience is as likely to cause relapse as an intensely painful experience."

Instead of embracing the feeling of vulnerability that attends joy, we are more likely to avoid the vulnerability altogether with a counterproductive defense mechanism. In moments of joy, we begin to think of worst-case scenarios. Focusing on the worst-case scenario and not the joy of the moment, allows us to feel less vulnerable—because if the good gift is taken away—then we have already prepared ourselves ahead of time for this pain. Of course, the huge price paid for avoiding the vulnerability of joy is the pain of focusing on potential experiences of loss, most of which never come to pass in real life.

When I was sharing this concept in a gratitude seminar, a man named Henry exclaimed, "Now I understand what happened to me on my wedding day!" He went on to tell how after the ceremony he had the terrible thought of how painful it would be if his new bride were to die. He started feeling depressed. His wife asked him what was wrong, but he didn't want to tell her because he didn't want her to start thinking the same thing about him. He said it caused a real strain for them on their wedding day. Henry was the victim of his mind's defense mechanism designed to avoid the discomfort of joy. How much better to simply embrace the vulnerability of joy, trusting that you will be given the grace to deal with whatever losses may come in the future.

In addition to this, Brown found we tend to miss out on joy because we try to numb negative emotions. First of all, "there's no such thing as selective emotional numbing. There is a full spectrum of human emotions and when we numb the dark, we numb the light." Individuals who are trying to avoid the pain of feeling uncomfortable emotions, like vulnerability or sadness, may attempt to numb or avoid feeling these emotions. As a result, they are also numbing their ability to feel joy. This greatly affects the ability to feel gratitude as well. Whenever certain emotions are selectively avoided, all emotions will be diminished. Consequently, the willingness to feel uncomfortable emotions is essential to keeping a strong emotional range, allowing for deeply felt gratitude.

So, you need to ask yourself, am I trying to avoid feeling negative emotions? If so, that may explain why you aren't feeling much joy in your life either. When we attempt to numb one emotion, we end up numbing them all. I wish I could figure out a way to selectively numb only the negative emotions, but it just isn't possible. So, we must be willing to feel all of our emotions fully. The difference is that we can choose to let go of the negative emotions quickly after they have served their purpose. Then we can choose to savor positive emotions through the practice of gratitude, so they have a stronger effect on us. This will lead to a gratitude mindset and an overall feeling of being blessed.

But I cannot stress this one point enough: Gratitude is not an escape from pain. We must feel the pain in our lives. Gratitude ensures we don't get stuck there. The practice of gratitude allows us to move through our pain and come out on the other side with a sense of appreciation for having learned from it. Gratitude allows pain to become a part of our reality without becoming our only reality. If we try to run from the pain, it will eventually catch up with us and take us over.

I remember having to put this into practice at a crucial turning point in my life. I was trying to make a group of people change into something they didn't want to be. It was foolish on my part and created a great deal of conflict. As a result, there was a lot of pain in my life. I was used to people liking me, and now there was a group of people who were seriously upset with me. I felt like a failure professionally. I felt attacked personally. I felt frustrated and angry because I couldn't accomplish what I wanted to accomplish. I did my best to run away from all this pain, and the more I avoided it, the more depressed and overwhelmed I became. Finally, I realized I had to face it or go crazy trying to escape. I chose to face it.

Fortunately, I reached out to others for support during this dark time, and slowly I allowed myself to feel the pain in my life. I prayed and asked God for help. I began to find healing in my soul. I realized many of my problems were self-created because I had become so absorbed in this negative chapter of my life. I started to feel empowered when I recognized if I changed my own atti-

WILL JOHNS   39

tude, I could experience the exact same reality more positively. I didn't give up trying to change some of the outer circumstances of my life, but I realized I needed to accept what I could not change. This led me into a deeper awareness of the power of gratitude. I could find joy in painful outer circumstances by looking for the good and savoring it. As I started to feel more joy in my life, I became aware of my own fear. I wondered how I would cope if I lost that which brought me such joy. I realized out of defensiveness I had become adept at playing out worst-case scenarios in my mind, which robbed me of gratitude's joyful fruits. So today, I choose to feel all my emotions. And when joy brings an accompanying feeling of vulnerability, I choose to embrace the whole experience. It isn't always easy, but I am so much happier now; I would never go back to running away from discomfort.

How about you? I'm guessing you've probably never considered the idea that a part of you tries to run away from joy itself. But if you can now see this tendency, you have the option to do something about it. Next time you feel a deep-seated joy in your life, make the choice to embrace it fully. Savor the joy in the moment. Don't try to figure out how to box up the joy so you can control it. Just accept it for what it is and delight in it. In so doing, you will overcome obstacle number two.

A Sense of Entitlement

Now we are ready to tackle the final barrier: A sense of entitlement. When we think we deserve to be treated in a certain way, and then our expectations are not met, we are likely to feel resentment. Strong feelings of resentment are a barrier to the practice of gratitude. In fact, gratitude and resentment cannot coexist. The mind will either be focused on one or the other. The greater the sense of entitlement, the more likely it is such an individual will feel resentment instead of gratitude.

This occurs when the mind becomes so accustomed to a benefit, it no longer appreciates it. Watkin's research has shown how humans have an amazing ability to adapt to their ongoing circumstances: "In the context of emotion theory, Frijda (1988) referred to this as the "law of habituation." Briefly, this law states that, over time, we tend to get used to our current level of satisfaction. For example, a major league baseball player may not be happy (and perhaps may even feel deprived) with his $500,000-per-year salary, because this has been his salary for the past 5 years, and other teammates are making much more."

No matter our status or level of personal achievement, when we get used to the benefits we receive daily, we tend to take them for granted. Over time, we may even feel we deserve these benefits, and have earned them. As a result, we are no longer grateful for what's good in our lives, since these things have come to be expected. Rather, we get angry when one of these perks is removed. Even a very small annoyance, such as losing the television remote, can fuel anger and a sense of injustice. This is the danger of entitlement. It obscures reality. And it renders us incapable of fully appreciating all of the good we have in life. Instead, we become continually angered by the perception of benefits lost.

Wherever the bar of "normal" is set, we tend to only feel gratitude when someone or something exceeds our expectations in a positive way. Therefore, the more good things we have that are taken for granted, the more likely it is that resentment will result, since the odds of losing one of these benefits have increased. This explains how wealthy people can be miserable.

Does it mean having more is a disadvantage? No it does not. Fortunately, people do not have to succumb to the law of habituation. Gratitude provides a way out of this natural trap. If the mind is focused on how good things are, the law can be counteracted. In fact, the practice of gratitude is the only effective way to counteract the law of habituation. Consequently, when we let go of entitlement, we have the opportunity to use contrast to our advantage. We can begin each day with no expectation of deserving all of the benefits that we will receive. Thus, we are prepared to appreciate all the good gifts that come our way, and this leads most naturally to gratitude.

I don't know about you, but I have really struggled with this sense of entitlement. As I look back on my life, I have been given so much more than most people in this world. But I have struggled to fully appreciate all of the gifts that have come my way. Somehow, over time, the law of habituation took over and I began to take all of these gifts for granted. So, since I have enjoyed very good health for most of my life, I began to feel entitled to be healthy all the time. As a result, when I got sick, I felt a strong sense of resentment. I blamed God or beat myself up for not having a stronger constitution. In the end, it just makes everything worse. How much better to accept my illness and do what I need to do to get better. How much better to express gratitude for the health I enjoy most days and easily take for granted.

You may have noticed this entitlement in yourself when you experienced the COVID-19 quarantine. You were used to having the freedom to go where you wanted to. Suddenly, that was taken away and you probably felt frustrated by that. However, when you were allowed to go shopping or go out to eat again, you probably appreciated this much more than before the quarantine. Losing something can help us recognize its value.

Another entitlement I have wrestled with is expecting things to come easily to me. When it doesn't, I want to quit and give up. My sense of entitlement shouts at me, "This is too hard!" I feel like throwing my hands up and not trying. But if I can recognize I have been blessed to have many things work out easily for me—but I am not promised that everything in my life will be easy—it can help me exercise the patience required to accomplish certain things in my life. Once again, the practice of gratitude can help diminish my sense of entitlement and create a sense of humble appreciation for all I have been given. I still have to face my challenges, but with the right attitude, I can approach them with energy and excitement.

The most important thing for us to understand about the law of habituation is that if we are not practicing gratitude, we will actually become more dissatisfied with our lives the better everything goes for us.

Percent of things going well in my life

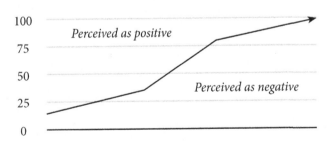

If you look at the chart above, you can see that the more things are going well in your life, the more likely you are to perceive something as negative because you are expecting everything to go well. When life is difficult, the smallest thing going your way can be perceived as very positive. The same positive experience will feel negative in contrast to all the good in your life as your life improves.

For example, when I was in college, I lived in a small dorm room. I slept on a very poor quality mattress on the top bunk. I shared this space with a roommate who would stay up working on a computer program until 3 or 4 a.m. I used a shower we cleaned only once a semester, and I vacuumed the floor at about the same frequency. When I would visit my parent's house, it felt like stepping back into luxury. I had a soft bed in my own clean room. I could take a shower in a clean bathroom. The contrast of my situations made everything feel very positive. However, today I have a mattress I really like, my master bedroom is kept clean as well as the master bathroom. My wife goes to bed at the same time I do. When I visit my parent's house now, I usually have a tough time sleeping the first night because it isn't what I'm used to. I experience the new space in a slightly negative way because the contrast is no longer in my favor.

The law of habituation guarantees money will never buy us happiness. At best, money can bring us temporary happiness that leads to long-term dissatisfaction. We need a spiritual solution to this law of habituation, and that is what gratitude provides. When we can thank God for all of the blessings we enjoy in our lives without any sense of entitlement, we are truly free to enjoy the good things in this world. The law of habituation will no longer push us towards resentment. Instead, we can delight in the simplest of blessings.

So, guess what? We have hurdled the final obstacle! How does it feel? I hope you are feeling empowered by this knowledge. Yes, the obstacles are significant, and you may wonder if you will ever make it, and that's ok. These are not obstacles that any of us will overcome overnight. But through paying attention, you can begin to get through these obstacles little by little on a daily basis. And soon you will build momentum and find you are feeling more and more gratitude every day.

Now that we are in the right mindset, let's take a good look at a large pitfall to which we can easily succumb if we are not careful—the negative story. If we get stuck in our temporary negative emotions, they can become a lens through which we look at our lives. And when we look through the lens of the negative story, we will soon be moving in the opposite direction of gratitude. So, let's make sure we understand how this process works, so it doesn't dominate our thoughts.

$$\int x = \frac{1}{-|x|}$$

CHAPTER 4
THE NEGATIVE STORY

I have struggled with perfectionism most of my life. Consequently, it isn't surprising to me that I held my parents to an impossible standard. My expectations of them were not realistic. I believed they should always think anything I did was great and always take my side in any situation. I expected them to love and nurture me perfectly so that I would always feel emotionally secure and good about myself. We probably all have longed for something similar from our parents or others in our lives. But for me, the big downside of these lofty ideals is that I began to resent my parents for falling short of my expectations. And I carried that resentment around with me. Even worse, it didn't stop with my parents. Anyone who dared to criticize me or didn't agree with me, I quickly began to resent as well. The resentment would come out in negative put-downs behind these individuals' backs. This is embarrassing to admit now. For many years, I was convinced that my parents had somehow messed me up for life. I wondered if I could ever be the person I really wanted to be. And that led me to a deep-seated resentment. However, when I finally started seeing some positive changes in my life—and began to realize the power to change was dependent on my choices, not my parents' choices—I became energized and willing to let go of my resentment. When I began to understand my parents had given me the best they had to give, it helped me become more compassionate, and my resentment melted away. It is infuriating to think someone has something great they could give you, but they refuse to do so. When I realized that my parents never purposely withheld some good gift from me, it set me free to accept them and move on. I was able to accept what they had given me with gratitude. This helped me to focus on the empowering thought that whoever I became in life moving forward was up to me.

In summary, resentment is based on the false perception that someone else has more power over my life than I do. When I give away my power by believing this lie, I will almost certainly resent the person I have given such power to. Think about it for a moment. If you believe others have the power to make you happy—but they consistently refuse to do so—you will definitely resent them! So, please follow me closely now. Gratitude is never a band-aid that we place over the large cancer of resentment and pretend it will fix such a serious problem. It just doesn't work! Gratitude is an empowering way of looking at your life that allows you to let go of the poisonous cancer of resentment. It is really a new way of seeing your life. It is also a new way of seeing everything else. Once you begin to understand that other people cannot control your choices, you are empowered to live your life in alignment with your deeply held values. Even in the worst possible situation, like the concentration camps of Nazi Germany, people have maintained their freedom. Victor Frankl, who endured the horrors of a concentration camp and lived to tell the story, wrote this: "Everything can be taken from a man but one thing: the last of the human freedoms—to choose one's attitude in any given set of circumstances, to choose one's own way."

Now, when we talk about resentment, we are talking about changing our perception of what other people do to us. However, if there has been some real pain in your life, that is not just a misperception of reality. We will talk about how gratitude relates to real pain in the next chapter. Resentment is not pain in my current reality. It is a negative story of pain that I continue to tell myself over and over again. Whenever my mind is focused on this painful story, I will feel the strong negative emotion that causes my mind to seek other negative situations in my life—which strengthens the negative feeling even more. I will begin to believe my future is bleak, because I am looking at it through the lens of my negative story. If this negative cycle continues uninterrupted long enough, I can find myself in despair—most likely turning to compulsive or addictive behavior in an attempt to escape. But gratitude is definitely the better way to break this vicious cycle of negative thinking. Here is a practical approach you can try next time you are feeling down in your life.

First, acknowledge to yourself that you are feeling bad. You can say something simple like, "I'm feeling negatively towards my boss right now." You fill in the blank where I put the word "boss." It could be anyone in your life. Next, ask yourself what this person did that sparked those emotions in you. But at the same time remember they didn't make you feel that way. In this case, you might say, "I feel resentment towards my boss when he moved my deadline up, and now I'm sure I won't be able to meet his expectations." The next step is crucial to this whole process. If you can answer this question, you will be amazed at how it sets you free. What is the story I'm telling myself about this situation? Take your time to really discern what feels true. In this case, you may be saying to yourself. "I'm going to fail at this project, and then my boss will see the truth that I'm really not good enough." Here is a helpful hint. Almost all the stories we tell ourselves, creating destructive negative emotions, come back around to believing that we are not enough. So, a spouse's criticism pushes the play button and we hear "I'm not good enough," accompanied by the strong feeling of resentment towards our spouse. Or our child throws a fit and we tell ourselves, "I'm a terrible parent," and we resent our child for "making" us feel this way. The good news is that once we can see the story we are telling ourselves, we can change that story. And that is guaranteed to change the way we feel.

So, whatever case you are thinking of right now, try telling yourself a different story and see what happens. In my example of the boss moving up a deadline, what if I told myself this instead: "I'm going to do my best to meet this deadline and trust things will work out in the end." This is a much more empowering story to tell myself. This story can completely change my attitude towards the project I'm working on and towards the people around me. I can begin to feel gratitude for the challenge I have before me, rather than despair for the overwhelming feeling of doom that the negative story focuses my mind on.

Let's work this through another example, just to make sure you are getting the concept. So, your partner criticizes you and you tell yourself, "I'm not good enough. I can't even keep my partner happy." This story is going to create personal pain and resentment towards your partner. However, if you can become aware of the story you are telling yourself, you can confront the story and replace it with a new one. So, what if you said, "My partner really cares about me and is wanting things to work well between us. I am grateful for the opportunity to grow and to learn how to love my partner more effectively." This is a completely different story than the one before. Notice how different you feel when you tell yourself each story. Think about how each story will affect your behavior moving forward. The "not good enough" story will lead to resentment, conflict, and more problems in your relationship with your partner. The gratitude story is energizing and will most likely promote positive action, moving your relationship into a better place.

I have a daughter that really doesn't like doing her Math homework. One day when she got home from school, I said, "It's time to do your Math."

She said, "No, I'm not going to do it."

I said, "Yes, you have to do it."

She said, "I don't care. I'm not doing it."

I sent her to her room and told her that she could come out when she was ready to cooperate and do her homework. She threw a huge fit. And it triggered a negative story for me. I felt like a terrible parent. But I used the technique that I have just shared with you in this chapter. I questioned myself. Is it loving to tell her that she no longer has to do Math? That would be easier for me but not better for her. Actually, my insistence that she do her homework is good parenting. I need to support myself in this. And so, my attitude changed. I still felt a little anxious about the conflict, but I persevered. Finally, an hour later, my daughter came down out of her room and said she was ready to do her homework. We completed it in 10 minutes. The next day on the way home from school she asked me if we could do her Math homework in 10 minutes again. I told her I thought we could. She didn't fight it at all. We finished her Math homework in 12 minutes and we both felt better.

This story illustrates how important it is to affirm our good choices, which don't always give us immediate positive feedback. It was good parenting to require my daughter to do her homework. But the immediate feedback triggered a negative story in me that caused me to feel like a terrible parent. So, I needed to question this story to find the emotional reserves to persevere. I needed to own the story as my issue and not blame my daughter for "making" me feel this way. I felt totally different when I affirmed myself for doing the right thing even though my daughter's behavior was the same.

This all stems from the truth that no one can make you feel a certain way. In reality, other people can push buttons that cause us to hit play on certain old recordings in our brains. It is these stories that create the painful feelings we encounter. So, take some time this week to put this into practice in your life. When you feel resentment, try to discern the story you are telling yourself and then replace it with a new and better story of gratitude. This one simple exercise has the power to significantly change your relationships with the people who are important in your life. Ultimately, your change of attitude has a huge influence on other people. For instance, when I was resenting my daughter for refusing to do her homework and "making" me feel like a lousy parent, I contributed to her resistance to my request. She could feel my negative energy being focused on her. That triggered her negative reaction to me. You can see how a vicious cycle develops here. But when I changed my attitude towards myself, I also changed my attitude towards her. She could feel this, and now I was encouraging her cooperation.

Once we learn how to discern the negative recordings that we play in our minds, we can begin to push the stop button and start telling ourselves a new story. This will greatly reduce the amount of pain we experience in life. The pain from our past will stay in the past and no longer be rehashed over and over again. Certain pains in our lives have probably been experienced thousands of times because we were not aware of how this process works. The next step for us is to learn how gratitude relates to real pain in our lives. It is essential to distinguish between real pain and the pain we cause ourselves by rehashing negative stories. Now that we can see the difference, we are ready to practice gratitude even in the midst of real pain.

CHAPTER 5

GRATITUDE AND PAIN

My world began to fall apart the day I accepted a call to lead a church. That very moment, I began to feel overwhelmed. It was so important to me at that stage of my life to be considered a "success." And now it felt highly likely that I might fail.

To make a long story short, I did fail—precisely because I was so consumed with "being a success." If I had simply loved and empowered the people there, it would have completely transformed the experience. But instead, I tried to change the people so that the church would grow, and I would get the credit. The members rightfully resented this, and so conflict ensued. And I didn't handle that well at all. It didn't help that I also told myself an, "I'm not good enough" story, which just increased my resentment. For a long time, I was convinced this was everyone else's fault. Finally, I summoned the courage to admit that it was my fault. I was the one who most needed to change. This whole situation caused me some very real pain. All my dreams of being a "success" were shattered, and I wasn't sure who I was anymore or how to proceed. I felt like I was falling into a black hole. I was anxious, afraid, full of shame and despair. These were all real feelings as I processed the fact that life was not going the way I wanted it to. Even though now I can look back at this time and be grateful for what I've learned from the pain, I am not specifically grateful for the pain itself.

I want to be very clear that gratitude does not attempt to cover over pain. It is not placing a band-aid on a broken arm and pretending everything is fine. Gratitude is not about telling everyone else you are ok when you are falling apart inside. Gratitude is not putting a fake smile on your face after a loved one dies. The grateful person must always look pain straight in the face without flinching. But that does not mean we are grateful for pain. I don't know how someone could be authentically grateful for pain. However, as I look back on my life, I am grateful for the things I learned by going through difficult experiences. Pain has served as a profound teacher. Pain has forced me to look at what was broken in me. And when processed in an appropriate way, pain can lead to transformation and healing.

I am very grateful for the transformation and healing I've gained from my pain. I can honestly thank God for these experiences. I would never seek the pain again or wish it on anyone else, but I recognize my pain opened me up to be willing to change and grow. Despair says, "This situation is horrible, it should have never happened. Therefore, all of life is horrible, and I might as well give up." Gratitude looks at the same situation, feels the same pain and says, "I don't like the pain I'm feeling now, so what can I do about it? What can I learn from this painful situation so that I can be a better person when I come out on the other side of this challenging time?"

Notice that the situation is the same in both cases, but the way the person looks at the situation is vastly different. And in the end, this changes the way pain is experienced. It is still difficult for both. But the lens of despair makes everything feel so much worse. For one, despair tends to create the feeling that the pain is forever and will never go away. The gratitude lens has hope built in by focusing on what will be gained through the pain when the worst is over. But gratitude never denies pain. Pain is real. Suffering is real. We cannot avoid it in this life. It is the price we pay for being alive in this world. Gratitude simply helps us deal with it more effectively.

As a pastor, I have had the privilege to walk with many people through the dark valley of dealing with the death of a loved one. This is real pain. It cannot be covered up or explained away. It can only be felt and eventually healed. I was trained to ask those who were grieving to tell stories about their loved ones. I could see firsthand just how therapeutic this was. The family would always smile through their tears when they recounted these memories. They began to connect in their minds that the pain they felt was in direct proportion to the real love they had for the one who had died. To have denied the pain would have been to deny their love. So, they learned to reflect with gratitude on all the ways that loved one had enriched their lives. They learned to thank God for each precious moment they had been given. And strangely, they found themselves able to feel gratitude and sorrow at the same time. It is a misconception that we can only feel singular emotions—so even in facing the death of a loved one—gratitude can help us find healing and joy in the midst of our grief.

Thankfully, we are not often facing major pain in our lives. However, gratitude is also extremely helpful when dealing with everyday annoyances and irritations. These are the more common, smaller pains—like getting caught in traffic, or having a difficult interaction with another person—which should also serve as triggers for gratitude. Thankfulness, once again, does not deny these painful moments in the day, but it also does nothing to add fuel to the fire of these experiences. The negative outlook would say, "Now my day is ruined!" and with such a statement, the prophecy is self-fulfilled. When the mind believes something to be true— even if it is not true in reality—it will still feel the emotions that correspond with the belief. Believing that traffic can, "ruin my day" will indeed ruin my day. Gratitude sees reality more clearly and more helpfully. Through the lens of gratitude, I can accept these situations for what they are without adding a negative story to them. I can say to myself, "I am stuck in traffic. This means I will be 30 minutes late." I don't add, unhelpfully, that being late is going to ruin my life. I accept the situation for what it is.

I was teaching about this in one of my gratitude seminars and one of the attenders, Bree, shared a recent experience that illustrated how gratitude can help with minor annoyances. She was terribly upset at the lawn mowing crew that mowed her yard. They consistently covered her sidewalk and driveway with grass clippings. She was thinking of calling their boss to complain. Every week they came to mow her lawn, she was annoyed. She told herself, "I bet they are doing this on purpose just to annoy me!" But after learning about the power of gratitude, she decided to approach the situation differently. The next time they were out mowing, she looked for the good in the situation. "I'm glad they are mowing my lawn for me," she thought. She reflected on the fact that they did a nice job cutting all of the grass. And she decided that she could just deal with the grass clippings. Except, when they finished this time, they didn't leave grass clippings all over her sidewalk and driveway as before. Did her attitude have any effect on them? I don't know. But Bree was amazed at how different she felt about the whole situation. Regardless of the grass clippings being there or not, she looked at the lawn mowers through a different lens and that dramatically changed the way she felt about them and the situation. I know I would be much happier overall if I chose to practice gratitude just like Bree when I'm dealing with people that may annoy me. This more accurate and positive view of people in general, allows me to perceive the real pain in my life more clearly.

By accurately seeing the pain in my life for what it is, I am able in moments of reflection to practice gratitude. I can look back over the day and still see the good that took place. I can say to myself, "You know, I got off to a rough start today by getting caught in that traffic, but I'm so grateful for the extra help I received at work from my colleagues who knew I was running behind. I was still able to enjoy some delicious food and when I got home, I had some great quality time with my spouse and children." This is the freedom gratitude brings. The freedom to still enjoy what is good in life, even when there is pain to be endured. Pain and joy. Both are always present. Gratitude allows us to choose to focus on joy. Our human nature tends to get stuck in the pain cycle. We fixate on unpleasantness, keep the pain cycle going, by telling the story to anyone who will listen. In addition, we tell the story over and over in our own minds. This is all to our own detriment. We are our own worst enemy.

The great news is we don't have to live like this. We can choose to focus our minds on what is good. We can balance our reflections of the day by acknowledging both the moments of pain and joy. This keeps pain in its rightful place in our lives—as a wise teacher. We do not let pain dominate our thoughts. We avoid telling ourselves a story that negates all the good in our lives. Let me give you an example: Matthew had a painful interaction with his boss at work. His mind began to race with thoughts like these: "I have to get out of here. That was too painful. I should never have been treated like that. I'm going to have to quit this job. Why do these bad things keep happening to me? I must be cursed or something. Now I'm going to lose my job, and my life is going to fall apart." Even if this story sounds a little far-fetched—if we examine what feels true to us in similar moments of pain—we can probably relate to Matthew's thinking. If we allow our anxious thoughts to take over, their downward spiraling narrative will obscure all the good in our lives. We are no longer able to acknowledge that good still exists, because, for us, all the good has been negated by our negative stories. In the end, Matthew recovered himself, worked things out with his boss, and had a great day at work the following day. So, his negative story was miles off from actual reality. Another reminder of the power of a negative story to distort reality.

This kind of negation story can form at any time in our lives, but is most likely to form in childhood. Someone may say, "Because I was born with an ugly body, I can never be happy." Someone else may say, "Because my parents didn't give me the love and support I needed as a child, I can never be happy." "Because my team lost the high-school football championship, I can never be happy." "Because the love of my life married someone else, I can never be happy." The list goes on and on. The content actually doesn't matter at all. All that is needed is the ability to recognize when one of these negation stories starts playing. When that happens, I would invite you to challenge the veracity of the story. Question the facts. Provide an opposing viewpoint. These negation stories successfully block out our joy, precisely because they are accepted without question. I can promise you will start to feel better about your life the minute you start questioning the "facts" of your negative story.

Get curious about what you feel is missing in your past. Ask yourself if it is something that still affects your present reality. If you missed the game-winning kick in high school, is there anyone in your life today still bringing it up but you? Probably not. That means it is only the story you are unnecessarily telling yourself that is repeatedly causing you pain. Liberation comes in rewriting the story. You could say, "I did my best, and it didn't work out, but that can't stop me from doing my best now." Nothing in your past is powerful enough to keep you from being grateful now.

This even works when life gets very difficult and scary. It doesn't mean that our problems go away. But now we have extra strength to face the challenges of life. This is how I've leveraged the power of gratitude one fateful day on the American River in Northern California. I was working at Leoni Meadows summer camp as the boys' director. I was given the privilege to guide a group of 12-14-year-old tween campers down a 23-mile stretch of the American River. Looking back, I can't believe they entrusted a college student like myself at the time, with this task. The River was running very fast and at twice its normal height that day. That meant that the typically class 3 rapids were now running in the class 4 range. I had already allowed my raft to hit Fowler's rock (generally if the rock has a name, you don't want to hit it!) which dumped us all into the water. By God's grace, we all made it safely back into the raft. But after running 22 miles of river safely, we had one final rapid to go through. The most daunting one of all, with the terrifying name of Satan's Cesspool. This rapid was a 7-foot drop into a churning pit of water. If you don't hit it right, you can end up spinning around in there for quite some time.

We were about a 1/4 mile away from Satan's Cesspool and I pulled my raft aside into some calmer waters. I saw a professional guide and I called out to him for assistance. "Excuse me sir, I'm wondering what the best way to run Satan's cesspool is for today, since the water is running higher." He looked at me and my tween campers and shouted back, "With your group, just bend over and kiss your raft good-bye!" What?!! That was not the encouragement I was hoping for! I saw the look of terror in the eyes of my campers. I had to do something. So, being the good theology major that I was, I said, "Let's pray." We prayed and I asked God to see us through this frightening rapid. And then I told my campers to take action. I said, "The minute we hit the top of the rapid you drop into the center of the raft. Stay in the raft, no matter what happens." Then the moment came. We were at the top of the rapid. Here is the picture from that day. The guy in the back of the raft with all that hair is me! What is going to happen?

We plunged into the abyss and . . . and . . . and . . . we came shooting out on the other side! Yes! I've never been so exhilarated! The tweens in my boat were so excited. I'm convinced, like me, they are still telling this story today. By focusing on our strengths, what we could do, we made it through a very difficult section of the American River. The previous picture captures for me how I feel about where I'm at in life at times. I have it prominently displayed in my office as a reminder of both the danger and adventure of life.

Gratitude and pain work together for our good. Pain lets us know that we need to tend to something important in our lives. Pain forces us to take stock of our feelings. Pain reminds us what isn't working in our lives right now. But gratitude keeps us from sinking into a Satan's cesspool of darkness in the midst of our pain. Gratitude, like my raft in the story, keeps us afloat when we suffer. Gratitude reminds us that not everything in our lives is bad. That we can still hope. That we have reason to endure the pain and to live another day. Dealing with pain without gratitude is the spiritual equivalent of running the American River without a raft. It could be done, but it wouldn't be pretty. Gratitude, like the raft, makes the experience of pain less painful. Gratitude keeps us from getting stuck in our pain.

It turns out that the practice of gratitude can relieve much of the needless suffering that our brains unconsciously inflict. As we become more and more aware of the stories we are telling ourselves, we will develop greater freedom to confront and change these stories, so that what we are telling ourselves builds resilience and increases our overall well-being. One specific way to do this is to let go of guilt. How can you do that? Let's dive in and see.

CHAPTER SIX

LETTING GO OF GUILT

If guilt isn't an issue that you've struggled with, I would encourage you to skip ahead to the next chapter. I share this specific chapter because I know that guilt can be a real problem for some people. Parents, for instance. I heard a report on the radio recently stating that parental guilt is at an all-time high. The focus for parents has increasingly shifted towards doing everything "right." Although I can't point to a specific study to back up this claim, it resonated with me. So, much research in psychology points to issues individuals have going back to childhood. As I've discussed in the previous chapter, this can create a victim story that we tell ourselves. "My parents messed me up, and now I'll never be what I want to be." That is a depressing thought! But as we become aware of these destructive patterns, it is possible to change the story to something much more empowering. "My parents did the best they could, and I am a stronger, better person today as a result of both their successes and failures." How is that possible?

Once again, we are looking at another benefit of the gratitude mindset. First, gratitude helps to focus our minds on the good that we received as children. In my case, I was given all of the most important basics in life and then some. I always had good food, a nice shelter, great education, and I knew that my parents loved me. Their rules were very consistent, which gave me a sense of security and trust. If you take a moment now to reflect on the gifts of your childhood, you may discover many benefits you had received that made you who you are today.

But the benefit of a gratitude mindset doesn't stop there. We can also see how some of the challenges of childhood—for which we may be tempted to blame our parents or in some cases are genuinely our parents' fault—also helped shape who we are today. Without the pain we experienced as children, we would not have the sympathy for others who also suffer. Some of you reading this book may have been abused as children and I want to be clear that I am not minimizing the very real pain that you had endured because of that. That pain was real. However, with support from others or professional help, that pain, when felt fully and let go, can be a source of creativity, compassion for others, and transformation in your life. Abuse should never happen to children. And it should have never happened to you. But you are far more resilient than you realize, and emotional healing is possible. Allowing your own pain to motivate you to show compassion to others is a part of that healing process. In that way, the pain can actually make you a better person.

No matter the degree of suffering you had endured as a child, it is important to remember that pain is a part of life we must accept. Even if your parents were perfect, you would still have suffered as a child. You would have still been angry when they denied you a second piece of candy. You would have still been upset when they told you to clean your room or do your homework.

All of this information about how crucial our childhood experiences are to emotional development makes anyone who is a parent highly susceptible to parental guilt. No other generation of parents has ever had so much psychological information at their disposal to assist in raising their children. But this mass of data can cause more problems than it alleviates. It can easily lead to more parental guilt. My brother was joking with me the other day that instead of saving up for a college fund for his children, he was saving for a therapy fund to help them undo all the psychological damage his parenting had inflicted! It is so easy when you are a conscientious parent to begin to feel you are damaging your children for life when you make even one mistake! That is intense pressure. Then to top it all off, we hang out with friends whose children are little angels—compare our children with theirs—and we feel even worse. We meet parents who are more structured than we are, more affectionate, more engaged in their children's lives, more proactive about taking their children to new and wonderful places, and we immediately feel like we have failed.

I heard another interesting report on the radio about the transition in the role of women in child-rearing. Back in the 50s and 60s, mothers who stayed home with their children were called "housewives." The primary focus of a housewife was keeping an immaculate house and making sure that her husband had a hot meal waiting for him the minute he got home from work. The children were not the top priority. Once they were old enough, they were generally allowed to roam their neighborhoods freely, and as long as they stayed out of trouble and didn't mess up the house, they were fine. Fast forward to today. Now a woman or man who decides to stay home with the children while their spouse goes to work is called a "stay-at-home mom or dad." The focus is entirely on parenting, and the clean house and hot meal at supper are often a thing of the past. The primary focus of both parents is the children and attempting to do everything "right" for them. You can easily see how this is a setup for increased parental guilt. And for many of you, this pressure has convinced you not to have children in the first place.

But parents aren't the only ones walking around feeling guilty. Social media has created an environment where we are constantly feeling "less than" others. We compare our lives to the photo-shopped images of our friends who are always having a blast and we feel like we are really terrible at life. We compare our internal misery to their external smiles, and we feel like losers. Five minutes on social media and we are viewing someone who is looking better than we are or seems to be having more fun than we are. It is a recipe for dissatisfaction.

So, regardless of whether you are a parent or not, this pervasive sense of "not doing it right" is deeply ingrained in our culture. The question is, how do we let go of this paralyzing guilt, always hanging around to point out our flaws and imperfections? Once again, you won't be surprised to hear me suggest that gratitude is the key to finding health in our self-expectations. The reason we feel the high level of guilt that we do is because we care about our lives and want to be the best we can be. Being a good person is an identity we wish to maintain. Therefore, our brains naturally zero in on any threat to this goal. Unfortunately for us, our brains are continually seeing new threats. It goes back to what we looked at in chapter 1 of this book. Our minds will naturally focus on the negative if we do not train them to do otherwise.

Let's go back to the example of the Spartan Race from chapter 3. If I had approached that race the way I often approach my life, I would have never finished it. I could not afford even a few seconds of self-criticism. I needed every ounce of energy I had to focus on the obstacle that was in front of me. And I needed every bit of encouragement that was offered to me by others on the course or from myself. Just saying "good job!" to myself after I completed an obstacle was a huge boost.

So, here is a simple and important new habit you can develop. Every time you evaluate yourself, make sure you focus on everything that you are doing well. For starters, affirm yourself for evaluating your life. That is step number one for becoming a better person. Good job! You've already got one thing on your list to feel good about. I was reflecting the other day that I needed to give more quality time to my children. I immediately felt guilty about this, which instead of motivating me to do better, simply paralyzed me and I did nothing. Fortunately, I decided that I also needed to affirm what I was doing well as a parent.

So, I reflected that I was providing well for my children financially. I was sending my children to good schools where they are interacting with great teachers who are instilling important values in them. I have done a good job giving them fun experiences that we shared as a family, such as going skiing together or camping or just for a walk in nature. I have taken them to many new and interesting places on vacation. I have modeled the value of hard work for them by doing my best. I had respected my teenage daughter's need for privacy and less time with me as she grows older and is more focused on her friends. My wife and I provided our children with a time of connection every day by sharing supper as a family. We had a family worship once a week. We made sure that we spent time tucking them in every night.

Now after listing all the things that were going well for me in this regard, I could see that I was already 90% of the way there! That thought was empowering, and now I can simply tweak the tuck-in time to be a little longer or look for opportunities where my kids come to me and request my time. Whenever possible, I can say yes when they suggest spending some time together. Now I have a plan that is doable. And I am excited about the opportunity to spend more quality time with my children.

But with the old guilt mindset, I felt paralyzed and the need to change felt like a demoralizing burden to me. Just by leveraging the power of gratitude to focus on the good as well as the needed improvement, empowered me to feel good about myself and to make a change for the better! It really is that simple. I challenge you to try this approach. It is a great gift that you can give to yourself. It is also a great gift you can give to your friends or family members when they are down on themselves.

As you learn to let go of guilt and to embrace a gratitude approach to your self-evaluation, it is time to add a couple more gratitude habits to your routine. Even if you only change this one habit—and always look at the positives of yourself every time you look at a needed improvement—you will feel much better! But there are more habits that can provide a boost to other areas of your life. Before we learn these new habits, there is one more essential principle that must be in place. We are going to address that now.

CHAPTER 7

START WITH YOURSELF

When I was 13 years old, my dad decided that he needed to get into better shape, and so he started running. He ran one to two miles once or twice a week. In his great zeal for his new commitment to health, he decided I needed to start running too. So one day, he announced I was going to run a mile. I was not happy about the prospect. What made it worse is that he decided he was going to follow me in the car while I ran. Why he didn't run with me. . . I didn't know. So there I was, running in front of the car while he called out my time and encouraged me to "pick up the pace!" I resented the whole experience and resisted running so strongly afterwards that he eventually gave up trying to make me run.

However, he did something far more effective. He stayed committed to his own workouts. Pretty soon he and my mom were running three miles, three times a week, a habit they have maintained for the last 30 years. I remember going running on my own a couple of times after that and enjoying how good I felt afterwards. Then I met a girl named Kelly, whom I liked, and she invited me to go running. She said, "I normally run 3-4 miles, is that ok with you?" I had never run more than a mile before in my life, but I wanted to impress her, so I said, "No problem!" From that point forward I have maintained a habit of running two to three times a week for the last 30 years. Recently, my ten-year-old asked me if he could go running with me. I told him, "Sure, let me drive behind you in the car!" Just kidding! I said, "Of course!" and we enjoyed a great run together.

I am grateful to my parents for instilling the value of exercise in my life. As a result, that value has passed on to two generations. Now my son is benefiting from a habit he observed in me, which I learned from watching my parents. More is caught than taught. If my parents had lectured me daily on the importance of exercise, but never actually exercised themselves, I am quite certain I would have resisted exercise as a result. But their positive example eventually won me over—with a little help from my friend Kelly!

Gratitude works the same way. It is much more likely to be caught than taught. At this point in the book, you may be so excited about what you are learning that you are sharing it with everyone you know. That's great! But let me caution you to beware of focusing too much on helping others become more grateful. The right time will come. But first, you need to fully develop strong gratitude habits in your own life and then you will have far more to share. The goal is for you to create a new habit of gratitude in your life. The great news is this: You don't have to be an expert in gratitude to benefit from practicing it. Just like exercise, you just need to do it.

Someone who has no idea how the body works but exercises regularly will always be in better shape than a medical doctor who understands the physiology of the body, but never works out. So, my goal is to get you to start practicing gratitude. If you do, you can be assured of immediate benefits. You can also be certain that your gratitude will be contagious, and everyone who is close to you will be more likely to start practicing gratitude themselves.

This is the most effective way to teach anybody anything. As a pastor, I used to fixate on trying to straighten out my congregation. I "knew" all the answers, and I felt strongly that if the people would just listen to me their problems would be solved. To my credit—I did attempt to practice what I preached—but one day I came to a devastating realization. My secret motivation for passionately preaching at my poor congregation was that I needed to try to change them since I kept failing to change myself. That was a humbling thought! But it marked the beginning of a transformation in my entire philosophy of influencing others.

I found through painful experience that the harder I tried to change other people the more they resisted me. Maybe you have experienced this as well? It happens with our children, our spouses, our parents, or even with our friends. The more we aim our efforts at getting them to change, the more they push back and refuse to listen. But thank God there is a much better way! This approach is much harder in the beginning and much, much easier in the long run. The truth is, the only person I can change, by God's grace, is me. When that happens, I will influence all others in my life. Systems theory tells us that when one part of a system changes, the whole system must change to compensate. I have found this to be absolutely true. Once this powerful truth began to hit home to me, I started to focus solely on changing myself whenever my natural reaction was to try to change someone else. The first thing I noticed is that my anxiety level decreased dramatically. I found out later that 90 percent of the stress we feel is caused by trying to control what we can't control. I don't know if you've discovered this yet or not, but I have finally realized that I can't control other people. I can influence them. But I can't control anyone but myself (and sometimes I don't do that very well either!). But what a relief to stop trying to control other people! Instead, if I found myself in a conflict with someone else, I focused on setting good boundaries and did my best to clearly communicate my opinion. How the other person responded to me after that was up to them. With my anxiety lowered, I started getting excited about the changes that I began to see in my own life. For so long, my efforts to change others felt utterly pointless, because those efforts were so terribly ineffective. Once I focused my energy on making changes in my own life, I began to see real progress, and that was very energizing!

Slowly, it dawned on me that this was working. People around me were changing. My wife treated me differently—in a good way! I was more effective at securing my children's cooperation. I enjoyed better relationships with everyone in my life. People would ask me questions about my experience and give me permission to speak into their lives and share my journey. The thing I longed to accomplish for so long was finally happening, but only when I stopped trying to make it happen. It was a paradox.

I know I have belabored this point, but it is human nature to want to change others before we deal with ourselves. Why? Because it takes far less effort on our part if someone else does the changing. But this approach leaves us unchanged. We must start with ourselves. If you want other people in your life to be grateful, you must not cram gratitude down their throats. It won't work. Whatever short-term gain you may see will be lost in the long term. Start with yourself, and you may not see much difference early on. But I promise, you will accomplish your goal in the end. You will pass on the value of gratitude to the people closest to you if you commit to your own practice. So, let's get started building new habits of gratitude.

BE GRATEFUL

CHAPTER 8
BUILDING GRATITUDE HABITS

Lauren had been struggling with some major health problems for several years. She went to many doctors in an attempt to pinpoint a diagnosis. She finally realized that she needed to make some major changes in her life and decided that she was going to exercise on a regular basis. She decided to start by walking around the block. On the first attempt, she came home exhausted—but not discouraged. She encouraged herself by focusing on the good she was accomplishing. Soon, she could walk around the block twice with relative ease. Eventually, she was able to slowly jog for a couple of miles at a time and was less tired than she was when she first walked around the block. Her incremental progress spurred her on, and this became the cornerstone of her physical healing.

Gratitude is like exercise. You don't have to understand how it works to know its benefits. You just have to do it. Like Lauren walking around the block for the first time, you could approach a gratitude practice with no desire to do it, and still reap the rewards. That is how powerful the practice of gratitude is! But it is far better to make the choice to practice gratitude because you really want to. Sometimes you just need a little motivation.

The point is this: whatever you have to do to motivate yourself to practice gratitude, do it! If you need to find a friend to share your gratitude with on a regular basis, do that. If you want to join some kind of gratitude group online, do that. Or even use social media to challenge yourself to post one thing you are grateful for every week. Whatever gets you started is going to help because once the habit is formed, you are going to feel so much better you will want to continue the habit no matter what.

Again, if you are impatient and just decided to jump to this chapter, like exercise, you can benefit from practicing gratitude with no understanding of how or why it works. However, the more you understand about how your body works, the more effective you can be with your exercise routines. The same is true for gratitude. The more you educate yourself, the better you will be able to practice gratitude with effectiveness. So, the remainder of this chapter will examine gratitude practices that have been proven effective in achieving these life-changing results. You should discover at least one practice that you can implement with a basic understanding of how it works. So, as you read the practices listed below, start with one. At some point, you may wish to try them all to see what works best for you, but, in the beginning, it's important to focus on the achievable. Here are the practices we will focus on in the pages below:

- Taking a gratitude walk
- Sharing gratitude with someone else
- Prayers of gratitude
- Remembering the difficult times
- Writing down your gratitude
- Telling a gratitude story

Before we get to these practices, we need to lay some groundwork to most effectively support your new life habit. The first step is making a conscious decision to become a grateful person. Choice determines what the mind is going to focus on, which in turn determines whether one will feel either grateful or resentful. The power of making a determined choice to become a grateful person is that it sets the intention of the will towards gratitude. This makes it far more likely that the practices of gratitude will be engaged on a regular basis. Choosing gratitude also prepares your mind to perceive more things you can be thankful for. If you are a person of faith, you will want to make this choice a part of your prayer life. You can ask God to help you turn more intentionally toward gratitude.

Now that your intention is set, you can begin to look for ways that you are already practicing gratitude in your life. Maybe you share some good things going on in your life with a friend. Maybe you listen to music that uplifts your spirits. Maybe you offer a short prayer of gratitude in your daily routine. Wherever you are already practicing gratitude is the place to start. Congratulations! You are already moving in the right direction. Now ask yourself how you could increase or build on your current practices. Simply getting more intentional about what you are already doing is a highly effective way to reinforce your new intention.

Next, you need to tweak your environment to help you out. A simple way to do this is to put reminders on your smartphone calendar to pop and say, "be grateful." There are also apps for this, I know of one called "Grateful." It's nice, because you can record your gratitude for later review. In addition, you can put a sticky note on your mirror that says, "I have so much to be grateful for." By making these small adjustments to your environment, you are directing your mind to focus on gratitude without using up precious willpower in the process. We only have so much energy to devote to the many decisions we have to make in a particular day, and only so much willpower to make the best ones. That's why creating these automatic prompts and setting environmental cues is crucial to supporting a change in your life. You don't want other areas of your life to suffer in the creation of this new gratitude habit.

Creating a gratitude habit is our goal. Ultimately, thankfulness should run on autopilot, and become the default state of our minds. Once you get to this point, it will not require any amount of willpower to practice gratitude. Gratitude will become a way of life for you, an attitude that pervades your mind throughout your day. This is the ultimate goal I have for myself, which, admittedly, I have not yet achieved. But that's ok because I had to start somewhere. I hope you will decide to make gratitude an ongoing habit in your life as well.

A habit consists of three parts, (1) cue; (2) routine; and (3) reward. So, let's look at how this might work in your situation. Imagine you have decided to practice gratitude right before you go to bed at night. (This is a great plan, because gratitude puts your mind into a positive, non-anxious state that promotes better sleep). The cue in this case would be getting into bed. The routine is to now practice gratitude once you get into bed. In our example, you could say a short prayer of gratitude for at least one thing you appreciated in your day. Then the reward kicks in because you will start to feel better and experience other benefits of gratitude in your life. Initially, this process requires a lot of willpower and maybe some reminders, like a note on your nightstand that says, "What am I grateful for today?" But over time, if you can stick with this for several weeks, it will become a habit that no longer requires any willpower at all. It will be automatic.

Once you set your intention to practice gratitude, tweak your environment to encourage yourself to practice gratitude, and plan how to form a new habit of gratitude, you are ready to choose your gratitude practice. I would encourage you to pick what sounds most appealing to you. Look for an internal desire that draws you towards one of the practices that I share with you. And finally, always start with small steps. Do not attempt to get up two hours early to write in a gratitude journal. That's way too much willpower, and I can promise you that such a large-scale change is unsustainable. You'll quit the practice after a couple of days and even worse, you may wrongly tell yourself, "Well, I guess I just wasn't cut out to practice gratitude." So, make your first step feel very easy and doable. The good news is no matter how small the practice, you will still benefit. So, I'm going to recommend five minutes to get you going. If you end up spending more time than that, great! But five minutes once or twice a day is something anyone can do. Later on, if you want to do more, you can simply increase the time, but the hard part of forming the habit will already be done.

Let me give you an example of how effective small steps can be. Three years ago, I set my intention to get into better physical shape. I had stopped working out for a while and my shoulders were especially weak and sore a lot of the time. I talked to my brother who was in much better shape than me at the time, and he gave me some helpful exercises that I could use to improve my shoulders. He told me to grab two weights to hold by my side and then raise them so that my arms were sticking straight out to the side and parallel to the ground. He emphasized that I needed to start with a weight that didn't hurt my shoulders. Injury would just set me back even further. So, I tried a weight that I thought I could easily do, and it hurt! So, I tried a little less than that and it hurt too! It is embarrassing for me to admit that in the end, I had to start with my wife's super-light, three-pound weights. And guess what color these tiny weights were? Pink! Talk about a blow to my ego! It was somewhat discouraging, but I eventually developed a positive way to look at this. I could only move up from here! So, I did very light workouts for only 15 minutes twice a week. But I stayed with it until working out twice a week became a habit. Soon, I was working out more like 30-45 minutes twice a week. Sometimes, I would add a third workout. Now, several years later, I am able to do the same shoulder exercise with 20-pound weights and my shoulders feel much better. That is a massive improvement. So trust me, starting small is the best way to get yourself moving in a new direction.

Now we are ready to look at some of your options for practicing gratitude. This list is not comprehensive, but rather it opens up some general categories of gratitude practice from which you can choose to be as creative as you like. As you read over this list and the explanation of the practice, pay attention to what draws your soul towards one or two of the practices. What sounds like it would be really fun to do? What feels doable? What inspires you?

We will begin with the most basic gratitude practices:

- Taking a gratitude walk
- Sharing gratitude with someone else
- Prayers of gratitude
- Remembering the difficult times
- Writing down your gratitude
- Telling a gratitude story

Let's look at these practices one at a time.

Taking a Gratitude Walk

We will start by taking a gratitude walk. I have listed this practice first because it is one that has worked well in my life. I enjoy getting outside in nature and walking, and so adding the component of gratitude to this current practice in my life made sense to me. It is as simple as it sounds. While I'm walking, I simply ask myself, what am I grateful for? No item is too small. There is no need to filter my response to this question or force myself to say something I don't mean. I simply reflect on what I am thankful for in my life. Here are some examples that come up for me. I'm grateful to be alive and experiencing this moment outside. I'm grateful for the comfortable shoes that I'm wearing. I'm grateful for my family and the opportunity I have to spend time with them. I'm grateful for the beauty of nature that I'm enjoying in this moment. I'm grateful for the feeling of breathing fresh air. In as little as five minutes, I can feel much more positive inside as a result of this practice. It is also a great time to reflect on what really matters in my life, which helps me deepen my spiritual life.

Sharing Gratitude with Someone Else

Next, we have the practice of sharing gratitude with someone else. This practice may feel a little strange at first. Most of us tend to share our negative experiences with others with the intention of gaining their sympathy and support. So, this is a new way to approach other people and, in the end, most people will probably appreciate the change. So, next time you are wanting to share with a friend how rude the waiter was when you went out to eat, try sharing how delicious the food was instead. When you want to share how scary the turbulence of the airplane was, share how grateful you were that you arrived safely. Sharing challenges with our friends and family is a normal and healthy thing to do, but when we add a gratitude practice to this experience, we are going to feel better ourselves and benefit our friends. Gratitude is contagious and it is a great gift to share with others. We have all met individuals who've lit up a room with their positive energy and gratefulness. These people energize and inspire us. They are a light in the darkness for us. We too can be that for others if we choose this practice.

I was visiting my 96-year-old grandmother last year in her assisted living facility and she introduced me to her neighbor who was 102 years old and the most positive person I have ever met. She looked 30 years younger than she was and she went on and on about all the things she was grateful for. I was truly inspired and decided that I want to be like her when I grow up! Committing to this practice of sharing what we are thankful for with others is the way to begin to become like my 102-year-old friend. Early on we may have to intentionally decide before meeting someone for dinner, "I'm going to share with them how grateful I am about _____" (You fill in the blank). I would encourage you to try this practice. The beauty of it is that it won't add any time to your day. You are going to talk to people anyway. Talk about your gratitude. You will feel better and your friends and family will all benefit as well. And if you are a parent, this is an essential piece to training your children to become more grateful. They are often listening to our conversations with others and they will catch on to the practice of gratitude themselves when they see you modeling it publicly. You can also share your gratitude with your children directly. Depending on their age, they may not be that interested but they will still be influenced by your positive example.

Prayers of Gratitude

I don't know what your faith journey has been, but I can be pretty sure that you probably pray at some point in your day. Research shows that over 90% of Americans pray and I'm assuming that percentage may hold true in other parts of the world as well. So, this is an excellent time to focus on gratitude. The ability to feel gratitude for what God has provided is one reason that spiritual people are more likely to experience gratitude. It allows them far more opportunities for gratitude than are available to others. So, think about all of the things that are currently out of your personal control and thank God for them. The planet earth is following its orbit at precisely the right distance from the sun to allow for your life to exist—that's something to be grateful for. Think of the big things that are easily taken for granted. The weather is beautiful today—it didn't have to be. What if we lived on a planet that was just warm enough for life but always cold, rainy, and miserable outside? A beautiful sunny day is a gift. Thank God for it.

The challenge for any of us who pray regularly is to avoid the trap of always going on and on about our requests. I need this, God. I need that. Please give me more money. Please keep me from getting sick. Please help my children to obey me! Requests are perfectly fine, but we will feel better if we can add gratitude to our prayer time. I believe that God is love and only wants what is good for our lives. God is for anything that makes our lives and the lives around us better and thankfulness definitely fits that criteria. So, the next time you say a prayer, make sure you start with some gratitude and you'll be feeling better in no time.

Remembering the Difficult Times

This next practice is going to seem quite strange as a gratitude practice. Aren't we supposed to avoid focusing on the negative? How could remembering the difficult times in our lives possibly help us become more grateful? Looking back at the difficult times in our lives helps us to clarify what really matters in life. When one of your children is sick, you recognize the deep-seated compassion that you have for your child. It helps you appreciate the deeper things in life and to be less annoyed by trivial matters. It also helps you understand how you can be strengthened through pain. Gratitude does not deny painful realities, but instead, it transforms the experience of suffering. Transformed suffering creates a sense of gratitude for the growth that has been gained through the challenging experience.

Most of us can look back at some of the very difficult times in our lives and see how we have become a better person as a result. Also, the law of contrast guarantees that we will be less likely to take our current blessings for granted when we remember how challenging our lives have been at certain points in the past. We may be living the dream right now that we have hoped for many years ago. I remember a time when it felt like everything in my life was falling apart. I was struggling at work, my relationships with my wife and children were strained and I wondered if I would ever make it through this difficult period of my life. As I look back now, I feel tremendous gratitude because I can see that God used this difficult period in my life to help me grow into a more compassionate person. I can also be thankful that I am no longer facing those same challenges today. Many things that seemed hopeless to me at that time are working out for me today. This is an example of the power of remembering our difficult times as a gratitude practice.

Writing Down Your Gratitude

The practice of keeping a gratitude journal is proven to be the surest way to experience the benefits of gratitude in your life. It is also the most difficult practice to maintain. The only reason it is difficult is that it will require time and discipline to maintain this practice. If you already keep some kind of journal or diary, then you can simply start adding gratitude to your entries. Or if you like to post things online, you could focus those posts on gratitude. If you don't currently do much writing—this practice, though guaranteed to be effective—may not be for you. It is kind of like the equivalent of running 10 miles a week. That is guaranteed to get you in good shape, but most people aren't ready to start their workout at that level. So, don't be hard on yourself if you attempt this practice and find that you are not able to maintain it. If you are looking for the most doable way to start practicing gratitude, I would certainly choose another practice.

However, if you are really pumped up about being more grateful and you want to see results right away, this may be exactly what you are looking for. This practice is as simple as it gets. Get a pen and paper and write down what you are grateful for. Think of anything that comes to mind, no matter how small or mundane. Here is one woman's list to give you an idea:

"Bath soap. Toothpaste. Hot water. Dishwashing detergent. Air conditioning. Houseplants. Sunsets. Sunglasses. Birthday cards. Blue skies. Flashlights. Blankets. Family Photos. Fresh fruit. Measuring cups. Warm clothes. Books. Bookcases. Beautiful music. Clean sheets. Autumn leaves. Sticky notes."

The practice is actually more effective if you are able to recognize all of the little things. If you go for large categories like life, friends, health, etc. you will quickly run out of things to be grateful for and will end up taking a lot for granted. The writing process focuses your mind and will help you hone in on all of the specific ways that you are blessed. I believe this practice is especially effective when it is difficult to feel grateful. If you can force yourself to write down a few items of gratitude, it can help you start to feel better right away.

Telling a Gratitude Story

Finally, we have what I believe to be the most powerful gratitude practice of all. This practice is really the culmination of all of the other practices. It is about the story you tell yourself about yourself. Ultimately, we really have only two choices for this story: We can choose to label ourselves either "blessed" or "cursed." This choice is extremely important, because whichever label we choose, our brains will take the cue to expend our energies to fulfill that belief. So, if I decide to label myself as "cursed," I will begin to make choices that guarantee that my life will not go well. Most people will not even be aware that they are fulfilling a label that they have given to themselves. They will simply just keep reinforcing the label by telling themselves, "I must be really cursed!" For example, the parent who believes they are cursed will often only see their children's flaws. When their children make messes, they will sigh with resignation and say, "I guess I'm just doomed to pick up after them for the rest of their lives . . ." Instead of creating a budget, the person who struggles financially and believes they are cursed will say, "I'll never have enough money . . ." The belief in being "cursed" is one of the most fundamentally damaging beliefs that a person can maintain because of how powerfully self-fulfilling it can be. In fact, even when things go well for the person who believes they are cursed, they will do something to sabotage their success. So, they might land a great job and then two months later quit because "My boss was a jerk!" Now they can continue to call themselves cursed. If you think you may have fallen into this trap, don't be hard on yourself. Just embrace this good news. You are not cursed! Let that sink in for a moment. Challenge your old thinking and let go of this life-draining, soul-killing belief. See it for what it is. Just a belief.

The reason this belief is so dangerous is that when your mind embraces a belief, your mind will automatically look for all the ways it can confirm this belief. Think of your belief as the seat of a stool. Once the seat is in place, the mind looks for supporting evidence—the legs of the stool—in order to keep that belief in place. If you believe you are cursed, you will have no end of evidence to support this claim because your mind has already found it for you. Your mind is probably doing that to you right now. When I say, you are not cursed, what comes to mind? Is your mind saying, what about this? What about that? Those were terrible things that happened to me. I'm definitely cursed! If so, then you have a first-hand example of what I'm talking about. So, I'm going to challenge you right now to question this belief. Let's remove the supporting evidence by getting your mind to focus on a much better and truer belief. You are blessed!

Even if you are still skeptical, go along with this exercise. Just let yourself believe that this statement is true for the next 10 minutes. You are blessed. Now, I want you to provide yourself with the appropriate supporting evidence. Go ahead and write down three ways in which you know for a fact that you are indeed blessed:

1. _____

_____

2. _____

_____

3. _____

_____

Notice something powerful. How do you feel right now? I am almost certain you are feeling more empowered. This is the highest leverage practice of gratitude that I know. To live each day with the belief that I am blessed focuses my mind to search for all of the ways that this belief is true. And when I do that, I come up with all kinds of good evidence in my favor. But the opposite is also true. I can find tons of evidence to prove that I am cursed if I so choose. But for what reason? What is the benefit in that?

Ok, I know what you are asking now: So, if I can selectively find evidence for being blessed and for being cursed, then isn't it true that I am neither blessed nor cursed, but that I am both—depending on what is happening to me in the moment? The answer to that question is no. It is true that both good and bad things will happen to you in this life, but the beauty is that you get to decide how you are going to define yourself through the ups and downs of life. You get to decide what label you want to slap on your own forehead. You get to decide that you are blessed, and you can train your mind to look for the evidence in your favor. If something bad happens to you today, that doesn't negate all of the good that has happened to you in the past. And something bad happening today, doesn't mean that nothing good can happen today alongside of it. Life gives you both blessings and challenges, but those things don't define who you are. You get to decide who you are. You get to choose which label to give yourself—blessed or cursed.

Now let me remind you once again, gratitude is not a trick and not an escape from pain. Believing that you are blessed doesn't mean that you won't endure trials and challenges in life. No one gets a free pass from pain in this life. But certain types of suffering are optional, because they are all in our minds. And believing you are cursed fits into this category. You don't have to believe that. And when you believe you are blessed, you will soon be amazed by how many things start going better in your life. I can guarantee your relationships with others will improve because you will be more positive and feel like you have more to give.

Depending on your current beliefs about yourself, this practice may prove to be very challenging. However, I am convinced that if you start with the small, doable practices that feel easy to you, you will soon find that you can begin to believe more and more firmly that you are indeed blessed. And once you have that outlook, the gratitude practices will start to come even more naturally. Pretty soon, people will begin to experience you as a grateful person. And your life will be better than you ever thought possible!

CHAPTER 9

MAINTAINING GRATITUDE HABITS

In my late 30s, I was in the best shape of my life. The Spartan Race I talked about in chapter 3 had inspired me to really start training and do more races. I decided to sign up for a super Spartan. It was 9.5 grueling miles up and down the mountainside of a ski resort, including 30 obstacles that challenged my core strength, upper body strength and ability to maintain intense exertion for a short period of time. I was proud of myself for completing this race with a time that was in the top 20% of the field. But after the race was over, I felt really tired. I didn't have any other races scheduled and winter was coming. I began to take things a little easier over the course of the winter months. It is clear to me now, that I slipped into some comfortable habits that did not help me maintain my excellent fitness level. I needed to be honest with myself that the training I did in preparation for the Spartan race was not something I could maintain over a long period of time.

However, I knew that I could do much better than I did after the race was over. The sweet spot for me is somewhere between my Spartan training and my winter slacking off.

The same principle holds true for maintaining your gratitude habits. Early on you may feel very enthusiastic and start five new gratitude habits at once. However, that is probably more ambitious than you will really be able to maintain long-term. In reaction to it, you may not do much of anything concerning gratitude for a while. That's ok. Be gentle with yourself as you are learning what your sweet spot is. Start small and build up from there. Always leave yourself wanting to spend more time in gratitude. Overdoing it is actually the surest way to lose all of your momentum. So, pick one gratitude habit to develop and commit to this habit no matter what. Get very certain in your mind that you are going to do this—no matter how difficult it feels. After two months, practicing this new habit should be automatic. It will be like brushing your teeth or combing your hair. It is just something you do each day. And this is where it gets good. You will be reaping the benefit of this habit without expending any extra effort or energy. Your brain will naturally focus on what is good in your life because a habit has been formed.

Maintaining the habit is simply a matter of making sure that you never let your baseline practice of gratitude slip into nothing. Let's say you decide to write down three things you are grateful for as you turn in to bed each night. After a while, this becomes a habit. It is just what you do. Then you decide to share those things with your close friends, your spouse, and your children when you talk with them. Now you are expanding your practice above the baseline habit you have chosen for yourself. This will take extra effort for a while until it also becomes a habit. From this point, you could choose to expand even further by reflecting on what you are grateful for when you go walking in the morning. Now, you have a very robust gratitude practice. You are noticing the difference it is making in your life and you feel more energized and productive in your life as a whole. How do you keep this going? That is a question you will need to answer for yourself, but let me share a few tips as you figure out what is going to work best in your life.

For starters, be aware of the possible temptation to do too much. You are probably doing too much when you are constantly pushing yourself to "get all your gratitude in" for the day. Once gratitude starts feeling like a duty that you have to do, you are probably heading for a pendulum swing in the opposite direction. It is like the person who commits to an extreme diet and loses 5 pounds in one week and then is so exhausted by the effort of this diet, they gain 10 pounds in the next month. So, keep an eye out for any kind of practice that requires unsustainable amounts of willpower. If your practice involves too much change all at once, it will very likely fizzle out. Start with what you know you can maintain. Remember my three-pound weights! That's where you have to begin.

Secondly, watch out for energy-sapping life events that can derail your practice. If you get the flu for two weeks, that could be an easy time to lose all of your practices. This is why choosing a baseline practice that you are going to do—no matter what—is so important. If you fight for your baseline practice, you will be able to maintain it in the midst of difficult times. In fact, you will begin to realize that you need it more in your difficult times. So, if you get busy, and you don't have time to walk in the morning for a couple of weeks and you lose out on that particular gratitude practice, don't sweat it. As long as you have your baseline practice in place, missing out on bonus practices is going to be ok. However, this is the time to double-down on your commitment to your baseline practice. Don't ever let your baseline get to zero. Five minutes is exponentially better than zero minutes a day spent on a gratitude practice.

Finally, watch out for boredom. You may find that when your life is going well and things are definitely better because of your gratitude practice, that you take these gifts for granted and get bored with your practice. In the mindset of boredom, you may ask yourself, "Why am I doing this?" If you are not careful, you may end up back where you started without even realizing it. You

may not believe me on this, but sometimes in our human bro-
kenness, we desire drama in our lives. We get bored with our lives
when they are working out well for us, and we tend to sabotage
our success by letting go of good habits. So, pay attention to this
train of thought and be prepared to embrace the lack of drama in
your life as a good thing. The same broken part of your brain that
focuses on the negative naturally, may also crave negative interactions with others. If you find yourself wanting to get into a fight
with someone, ask yourself what you are feeling and deal with the
emotion directly. In my experience, creating drama with others
only makes life worse for everyone involved.

Think of maintaining your practice like building a cathedral.
This is a lifelong pursuit, but what you get out of it, in the end, is
who you are becoming. You are becoming a great soul through
this practice. You are becoming a place that others will be blessed
to visit. You are changing your family tree by instilling in your
children the values of gratitude and the ability to enjoy their lives.
You are becoming a person that others will want to be around.
You are becoming the person you always wanted to be. Is that
worth the small amount of discipline required to maintain a baseline gratitude practice? I think so! Now let's celebrate all the benefits of this new way of life!

CHAPTER 10
ENJOYING THE NEW LENSES

I recently bought a new car. Actually, it is a car that is new to me but already used quite a bit with 140,000 mostly-highway-miles on it. This car was very well-maintained and having been recently detailed, it feels almost brand new. I am really enjoying driving this car because the experience is new to me. Also, because the car is so much nicer than my old car, since it is almost 10 years newer (the law of contrast). As a result, I am naturally grateful for this car. I appreciate the joy of driving it. I don't have to force myself to be grateful for it. I just am. But I now know the way my mind works and I know that pretty soon I'll lose interest in the car. It will soon just become a way to get from here to there. And I'll get frustrated with it when it breaks down and needs a repair. I'll be annoyed when I need to schedule an oil change for it and when I need to replace the tires. Eventually, the car is going to get old. I'm going to get tired of it. And soon, if I'm not careful, I won't appreciate it at all.

Why am I talking about cars in this chapter? The same process that will naturally happen to me regarding my new car is likely to happen to you as you currently enjoy looking at the world through your new gratitude lenses. Assuming that something you have read so far has clicked for you, then you are most likely now seeing the world in a new light and enjoying it. I am excited for you! However, this chapter is both a warning and a challenge for you. The warning is that you can easily fall back into old habits and no longer enjoy the benefit of living a grateful life. It won't happen overnight. But slowly, over time, the message of the culture around us is constantly fixing our attention on the "problems" of the world and what we don't have. Our own emotions get us caught up in family drama or anxiety regarding our work. Pretty soon, if we haven't developed gratitude habits, we can find that we are back to our natural state of focusing on the negative and not feeling very good.

I know this can happen because it has happened to me. I have spent years of my life studying this topic of gratitude and have more intellectual information on how to be grateful than I will probably ever need. But that wasn't enough for me. The information will only lead to transformation when I apply what I know and create life-giving habits that fill my soul with joy. This is my intention now. And I hope it is yours too.

So, here is my challenge for you: now is the time to decide to make the most of what you've learned. If you are feeling good—

and know without a shadow of a doubt that living a life of gratitude is what is best for you—then decide right now to make a plan to capture what you have learned. How do you do that? You must decide to make a gratitude habit. Set aside five minutes a day that you will use to both reflect on what you are grateful for and to evaluate how well you are practicing gratitude throughout the day. First thing in the morning or right before you go to bed are excellent times for this type of evaluation. Also, it is helpful to get a friend involved. If you have a friend who is willing to read this book and discuss it with you, make a standing appointment at least once a month to meet with your friend. Once a week would be even better! Meet for coffee, lunch, or simply to go for a walk and discuss how your gratitude journey is going. Share what is working and what is not working. Let your friend reflect back to you his/her perspective to help you fill in your blind spots. And of course, take the time to share what you are truly grateful for.

I know I have been spending a lot of time talking about the importance of establishing good gratitude habits. I have done so because it is the only way to benefit from what you've learned for the rest of your life. However, it may also sound like practicing gratitude is a ton of work when it isn't. Once your good habits are in place, gratitude will begin to flow naturally in your life. This is what I mean by enjoying your new lenses. You will start to become a grateful person and you will enjoy that state of being. It is who you are. Eventually, after years of practice, gratitude will become the natural state of your mind. It will be in the background—no matter what else you are currently focused on. When this becomes the case, you will find that you can fully enjoy silence and stillness. You will no longer be easily bored or become restless when the world around you isn't moving fast enough. You will experience the joy of being. Take a moment right now to sit quietly and feel the aliveness in your body. Cherish the joy of this moment. You don't have to resist what already is. You can accept this moment and trust that God has brought you to this moment for a reason.

Another way of thinking about enjoying the lenses is being grateful for the practice of gratitude. It is easy to forget what life was like before you had any gratitude practices. Like anything else, soon you can start taking gratitude itself for granted and fail to appreciate the joy and delight it has brought into your life. I am at the point in my practice now that I savor any moment where I am truly grateful. I know that I am still a long way away from being grateful all the time, so I am glad whenever it happens. And I have learned not to beat myself up when it doesn't happen. I remind myself that this is not a competition. I'm not trying to be more grateful than the people around me. I just want to benefit from the practice of gratitude in my own life. I also want the people close to me to benefit from my practice. I know that gratitude is contagious, and I want others to enjoy it as well.

Several years ago, I took my family on a trip to Smoky Mountain National Park in Tennessee. Overall, we had a really great time together there as a family. However, one night we decided to attend a magic show. When it was over, the magician demonstrated a magic wand that he had for sale. Two of my children wanted me to buy them this magic wand. I knew that if I did, they would tire of it in a matter of days. I also felt manipulated by the magician who made it look so great and then offered it for sale, knowing that all the kids would start begging their parents for one. I said "no" to my kids and my youngest daughter who was seven years old at the time started crying. We got in the car to drive back to the hotel and she started screaming, "I want a magic wand!!" I was quickly losing my patience. In a moment of parental hypocrisy, I yelled back at her, "Would you be quiet!?" It was a tense and awkward moment for everyone. After we got back to the hotel, I apologized to my children individually and to my wife for losing it in the car.

A few days later, as I reflected on the trip, I was feeling terrible. I just kept beating myself up for my poor parenting. Why did I lose my temper? Why did I yell at my daughter? Why do I get so irritable with my children sometimes? On and on and on. I felt awful. I felt like the worst parent in the world. I imagined my children signing up for years of therapy to cope with my horrendous failings. Then I had a thought that saved me. On that same trip, I had had an opportunity to teach a gratitude seminar. With the material I have presented in this book fresh in my mind from teaching the seminar, I asked myself, "What was good about the trip?" Then I was able to remember the Ferris wheel ride I took with my oldest daughter. I thought of the amazing hike we enjoyed as a family. The delicious food we savored together. The laughter, the bonding, the memories. There were so many good times. It was really a great trip overall. Yes, I had blown it as a parent for a few minutes, but I had also fulfilled my deepest values and had an amazing experience with my wife and children. Suddenly, I began to feel lighter. I felt hopeful and joyful. I was profoundly grateful for the entire trip.

My reflection on this trip became a metaphor for my reflection on life in general. It is true that negative things happen. I fall short of my ideals and that can be painful and embarrassing at times. But that is not the only thing that is true about me or my life. There are always other good things going on in my life. Wonderful things. Things that fit my values and delight my soul. And when I look at my life through the lens of gratitude, I can see both the good and the bad, the light and shadow together. I see the whole picture and the whole picture is far more accurate and far more hopeful than narrowing my vision to fixate on the flaws.

A negative focus creates the desire to throw in the towel and give up. I feel exhausted and hopeless and often fatalistic about my future. But through gratitude, I can begin to see all of the good things that are happening in my life and this feels so much better! When I see the whole picture, I feel empowered to do more good. I desire to be a better person. I believe that I can be the best version of myself. I know I will still fail and fall short on a fairly regular basis. But I also know that my failings aren't the whole story. In the long gaps between my failures, I can see so much good happening in me and through me. This is something I can be deeply grateful for. So, I invite you to put on your gratitude lenses and enjoy the new view. Even though nothing has actually changed in your life, everything will look different and that will actually change your life!

CHAPTER 11
GRATITUDE AND FAITH

*"Faith is a place of mystery, where we find the courage
to believe in what we cannot see and the strength to let go
of our fear of uncertainty."*

Brene Brown,

The Gifts of Imperfection

If you have stayed with me this far, you know something important about me: I am a person who deeply values my faith in God. I value my faith so much, I have dedicated my life's work to sharing this faith with others as a spiritual guide (aka, pastor). This spiritual journey is what led me to ultimately spend three years of my life studying the subject of gratitude. However, I waited until this point in the book to talk openly about my faith because I didn't want my faith to be a barrier to your journey with gratitude. I believe that you will benefit greatly from the practice of gratitude, even if faith is a struggle for you.

However, I need to mention what the research shows about the relationship between faith and gratitude. First of all, just professing faith in God or belonging to a certain religious group does not correlate with being more grateful. So, regularly attending worship services may be strengthening your faith, but it may not be making you more grateful.

That having been said, there are two distinct advantages to the person of faith who is attempting to be a more grateful person. First of all, the spiritual person has more opportunities for gratitude because he or she can thank God for things that otherwise would be seen as mere happenstance. I can thank God for a beautiful sunset or sunrise. I can thank God for the gift of life. For whatever health I enjoy. I can thank God for the beauty of nature, for the gift of music, and art. So, wherever you are at in your faith journey, I would encourage you to take advantage of how your faith can strengthen your sense of gratitude. If you are very strong in your faith, it is important to remember how crucial gratitude is to maintain a healthy and vibrant faith in God. Our tendency towards negative thinking can be very damaging to our faith. We can fixate on all of the ways in which we believe God has failed us somehow. Why doesn't God take away this problem from my life? Why did I have to go through that? Why is there pain in the world? Why is there pain in my life? Why haven't my prayers been answered in the way that I wish they were? Many people can end up losing their faith by focusing on such questions. Or they pollute their faith with such negativity that it becomes toxic and destructive to others. I don't believe these questions are bad in and of themselves, but if they become a focus, they can become a source of ingratitude. I would tend to look at these questions as confirmation that there is a power (God) that is much higher than me. If I were truly in charge of my life, then clearly, nothing would happen that I didn't approve of. In addition, the definition of faith itself means that I hold onto certain beliefs even when they don't feel true.

This is the second huge benefit of faith in relation to gratitude. If your gratitude practice is going to have any consistency at all to it, you will need to have some faith. Even though I am the author of this book, I have had moments when everything I have written seems to be false. It feels untrue. But my feelings about the topic don't make it true or false. They are just feelings. Faith allows me to step back and not to be overcome by my negative emotions. Faith allows me to take positive action, believing that my feelings will eventually follow my actions. Faith gives me the resources to endure hardship and difficult times in life, without concluding that all of life is hard and difficult. Faith allows me to experience joy in the midst of sorrow.

If faith has been a struggle for you, I would invite you to consider the role ingratitude may have played. For instance, is it possible that you have only looked at the negative side of religion? Maybe your experience involved attending a church that was boring and seemed stuck in the past. Maybe you encountered people who claimed to be loving people of faith but were hypocrites. Maybe you had negative interactions with judgmental fundamentalists who seemed to always be looking for ways to criticize your behavior or condemn you for your sins. Is it possible you have done the same thing with God? You have defined God by all of the suffering God has allowed in the world. How could a loving God allow this? But what about all the good in the world? Where did that come from? Was that a lucky chance or is there more to the story? And so, I would invite you to reconsider your faith in the light of gratitude. As long as you are only seeing faults, you won't be able to build much in the way of faith. Ingratitude leads to the dark pit of cynicism and despair. Trust me, I have gone down that path in my mind and it is not a path I would wish on my worst enemy. Focusing on the negative distorts reality and makes it difficult to make good decisions.

Let me give you some examples of how focus affects your faith. A while back, my wife and I were preparing to sell our home. I was cleaning walls that my young children at the time had marked up. I was scrubbing every mark I could off the walls with a Mr. Clean magic eraser. When my realtor came to look the house over, I asked him if I needed to clean some of the marks on one of the baseboards. He told me, "Don't worry about it. If they see that, they are not buying your house. Either they fall in love with your house or they don't. The marks on the baseboards make no difference." His comment has stuck in my mind ever since.

Here's another example of the same thing: My friend Kendra (not her real name) was dating a guy she really liked but she told me one day, "I can't stand the shoes he wears. They really irritate me." I knew in that moment that their relationship wasn't going to work. If something as minor as shoes becomes the focus of a relationship, it has no chance. Our brains are designed to find what we are looking for. If you are looking for faults with a house or a person, you will find them. If you are looking for problems with organized religion, Christian people, or God, you will definitely find them. You'll see the scuffs on the baseboard and the shoes will annoy you. But those details have nothing to do with the higher value faith can add to your life. If we focus only on the cost, we would never buy anything. If an irritating person walked up to me and asked me for $500, I would immediately say no. That's what happens when we focus on the cost. But if that same person had the latest iPhone for sale, I would gladly give him the money. That's focusing on the value gained.

Gratitude teaches us to acknowledge the cost, but focus on the value. What would it look like to evaluate a faith community through the lens of gratitude? If you decide you need the support of other people to help you grow in your faith, then you can try out some places of worship in your area. Maybe the first one feels too out of date. That's ok. Try another one. Find a place of worship that has a good feel to it. Find a place that has people you'd like to get to know a little better. And then focus on the value this practice can add to your life. Other people who have faith can support your faith in powerful ways. Even if you disagree with what other people share, it can help you clarify what you really believe. I feel strongly about this, because I have experienced firsthand what despair can feel like when life gets difficult. I know what it feels like to lose hope and I don't want anyone to go down that road if possible. I am so grateful for the faith I had in my life that saw me through so many difficult times.

One of the darkest times of my young life took place on a trip across the country. I was traveling with my girlfriend Jenny and my best friend, Jared (not their real names), and two other friends. Due to tensions on the road and the looming specter of a long-distance relationship fast approaching, Jenny and I broke up on the trip. The next day, she started to get together with Jared. I found out about all of this at a later time, but I felt what was happening at that time. It plunged me into a dark place. Who could I trust when my girlfriend breaks up with me and my best friend betrays me? I felt very hurt by the whole thing and overwhelmed emotionally. Then I arrived at the summer camp I would be working at all summer. I was there two weeks early and I did manual labor around the camp for 8-10 hours a day. It was a really tough time for me. I was lonely on top of everything else. But that quiet time of manual labor began to strengthen my faith. I had a sense that I was somehow going to be ok. It felt like I had just learned a very important lesson in life. I had hope that there were still some really good times ahead for me. I can't explain where that hope came from except by saying it was a gift of grace from God. That hope sustained my spirit and I began to take positive action throughout the summer to heal my heart and soul. And within a couple of years, I had met the woman who would become the love of my life from that day forward.

I have now been married to my beautiful wife Lori since May of 2000 and we have three amazing children. As I look back now, I am grateful for that painful time in my life. I wouldn't wish it on anyone, but I'm glad I learned what I needed to learn from that experience. I'm glad I learned that even when life looks darkest, there is always hope that I can cling onto with faith. That hope allows me to see the good things that are currently happening in my life alongside of the challenging things that are happening.

So, wherever you are at in your faith journey, I am quite sure that if you decide to take the practice of gratitude seriously, you will begin to see your faith in God strengthened and that faith in turn will help you become a more grateful person. I finished writing this chapter in April of 2020 when the whole world was processing the COVID-19 crisis. I was so grateful for the hope my faith brought me in the midst of tremendous uncertainty. The practice of gratitude played a big part in my ability to stay sane during that anxious time.

And so, I pray that your faith and gratitude will begin to grow and flourish to prepare you for whatever life may throw your way. It is my hope that starting with you and me, the world can slowly be filled with more and more grateful people to remind us all that there is always some light shining in this world, even in the midst of the deepest darkness. And I hope that collectively that light shows us how to take compassionate action so that this world becomes a better place.

CONCLUSION

I have a confession to make. For all of my knowledge of gratitude, I don't always practice it as much as I would like to. In this way, gratitude is like exercise. At a certain point, we no longer need any more information. We all know that we need to exercise. And you now know about the importance of gratitude. You know from research and your own personal experience that gratitude works. It really does help you feel better about your life. So, how come that doesn't automatically translate into being a grateful person? The answer is very simple: You have a choice to make every day. If you choose gratitude today, you will experience all of the benefits that go with it. If you continue to choose gratitude each day for the next 30 days, you will start to form a gratitude habit that can sustain you, even when you don't intentionally choose it. Action is what makes the difference. Making a choice! A series of choices in the direction of gratitude will ultimately build strong habits. Those habits will make it easier to choose gratitude on a daily basis.

And so there it is. What choice will you make today? Don't worry about tomorrow. You'll get another chance to choose gratitude when you get there. Gratitude can only be practiced in the present moment. One day at a time. If you deepen your understanding of gratitude, that may give you insight and inspire you to new practices. Further study on this topic can only benefit you. But it can't replace actually practicing gratitude in your everyday life. You can't choose gratitude once for all times. It is a daily choice.

Consequently, I invite you to put what you've learned in this book into practice. Decide to take action today. The knowledge you now have is like money in the bank. It has the power to benefit your life in so many ways. But if you never spend the money (put the knowledge into practice) you won't benefit from it very much. So, do it for yourself. Or do it for your spouse. Or do it for your children. Or do it for your friends. Everyone will benefit from you becoming a more grateful person. So, what are you waiting for? Your new way of life begins now.

ACKNOWLEDGEMENTS

I owe a huge debt of gratitude to the following individuals whose encouragement made this book possible.

Larissa Brass, who helped edit the majority of this book. I would have never got moving without your help, Larissa. You strengthened my writing in every way. I greatly appreciate your contribution to this work and your enthusiasm for the topic of gratitude. You practice gratitude better than anyone I know.

Jeanine Munoz, your encouragement early on, when I was just beginning to work on the book helped me get over the finish line. In talking with you, I believed that I could finish this, and it would be worth it. Thank you for believing in this project, and for all the guidance you gave to my project and thesis as I completed my doctorate.

Gordon Johns, you caught onto the concept of gratitude quicker than anyone I have ever shared it with. It still inspires me how you have allowed gratitude to change your life in so many amazing ways. Thank you for believing in this book and providing incredibly valuable feedback to guide the flow of ideas as they are contained here.

Jerry and Clara Lou Johns (aka Dad and Mom), you gave me a stable, loving home in which to grow and develop and explore life. I'm so grateful for all the gifts you gave me growing up. Thank you for instilling good health habits and good values in me. My life has been greatly blessed by those values. I am grateful your continued support.

Rick Johns, you helped to convince me that what I had to share was worth sharing. You reminded me that people will hear these ideas from me that might not ever hear them from someone else who may be more qualified to teach on this subject. It was that belief that kept me moving forward and helped me to get this book completed. Thanks for your on-going support and encouragement.

Lori Johns, you have supported me from the very beginning of this journey. You took care of our small children while I was away for my one-week doctoral intensives. You cheered me through the completion of my doctorate and attended my graduation. All of this I greatly appreciate. And you helped me clarify the overall approach to this book. Thank you for all the love and support you have graciously given me over the years. The more I practice gratitude, the more I realize how much I can thank God that you are in my life!

ENDNOTES

Introduction

Page 9.

Dr. Kelly McGonigal, "The Neuroscience of Change," April 19, 2012,

Sounds True: Insights at the Edge Web site, Mp3 file, 46:37,

http://www.soundstrue.com/podcast/the-neuroscience-of-change/?#bottom

(accessed September 16, 2012).

Page 10.

Robert Emmons and Michael McCullough. "Counting Blessings Versus

Burdens: An Experimental Investigation of Gratitude and Subjective

Well-Being in Daily Life." *Journal of Personality and Social Psychology*

84, no. 2 (2003): 377-389.

Chapter 1: Changing the Lens

Page 14.

Dr. Kelly McGonigal, "The Neuroscience of Change," April 19, 2012.

M.A. Killingsworth and Daniel T. Gilbert, "A Wandering Mind Is an

Unhappy Mind," *Science 12* (November 2010): 932.

Page 15.

Rollin McCraty and Doc Childre, "The Grateful Heart: The Psychophysiology of Appreciation," *The Psychology of Gratitude*, edited by
and Michael McCullough and Robert A. Emmons (New York: Oxford
University Press, 2004), 241-242.

Chapter 2: The Benefits of Gratitude

Page 22.

Emmons and McCullough, "Counting Blessings," 388

Page 23.

Emmons, Robert A. *Thanks!* (New York: Houghton Mifflin Company,
2007), 34.

Page 23.

Emmons and McCullough, "Counting Blessings," 388.

Page 24.

Philip C. Watkins, "Gratitude and Subjective Wellbeing," in The Psychology of Gratitude, ed. Robert Emmons and Michael McCullough
(New York: Oxford University Press, 2004), 172-174.

Page 25.

C.S. Lewis, *Reflections on the Psalms* (New York: Harcourt, Brace, 1958), 94.

Page 26.

Cloud, Dr. Henry. *Integrity* (New York: Harper, 2006), 106.

Chapter 3: What Gets in the Way?

Page 30.

McCraty and Childre. "The Psychophysiology of Appreciation." 241-242.

Page 31.

Roberts Roberts. "The Blessings of Gratitude." In *The Psychology of Gratitude,* edited by Robert A Emmons and Michael McCullough, 58-80. New York: Oxford University Press, 2004, 70.

Jean-Pierre de Caussade, *The Sacrament of the Present Moment* (New York: Harper Collins, 1989), 58.

Page 35.

Brené Brown, *The Gifts of Imperfection* (Center City, MN: Hazelten, 2010), 72-73.

Page 36.

Brown, *The Gifts of Imperfection*, 72-73.

Page 40.

Watkins, "Gratitude and Subjective Wellbeing," 176.

Chapter 4: The Negative Story

Page 48.

Frankl, Victor. *Man's Search for Meaning*, 66.

Chapter 8: Building Gratitude Habits

Page 81.

Chip and Dan Heath. *Switch*. New York: Broadway Books, 2010, 181-182.

Page 82.

Charles Duhigg, The Power of Habit (New York: Random House, 2012), 72.

Page 91.

Nancy DeMoss, *Choosing Gratitude* (Chicago: Moody Publishers, 2009), 113.

Chapter 11: Gratitude and Faith

Page 109.

Brown, *The Gifts of Imperfection,* 72-73

Page 110.

Robert A. Emmons and Teresa T. Kneezel, "Giving Thanks: Spiritual and Religious Correlates of Gratitude," *Journal of Psychology and Christianity* 24, no. 2 (2005): 146.

AUTHOR'S NOTE

If you would like to contact me, please do so at Dr.Will.Johns@gmail.com. I would enjoy hearing how the book has affected your life. Your feedback will help inform how I share this material with others in the seminars that I teach. For more information about upcoming projects that I am involved in, please visit: www.facebook.com/Dr.Will.Johns

Made in the USA
Monee, IL
15 May 2022